Positive
Provocation

Positive
Provocation

25 QUESTIONS
TO ELEVATE
YOUR COACHING
PRACTICE

Robert Biswas-Diener

BK
Berrett–Koehler Publishers, Inc.

Berrett-Koehler Publishers, Inc.
1333 Broadway, Suite 1000
Oakland, CA 94612-1921
Tel: (510) 817-2277
Fax: (510) 817-2278
www.bkconnection.com

ORDERING INFORMATION

Quantity sales. Special discounts are available on quantity purchases by corporations, associations, and others. For details, contact the "Special Sales Department" at the Berrett-Koehler address above.

Individual sales. Berrett-Koehler publications are available through most bookstores. They can also be ordered directly from Berrett-Koehler: Tel: (800) 929-2929; Fax: (802) 864-7626; www .bkconnection.com.

Orders for college textbook / course adoption use. Please contact Berrett-Koehler: Tel: (800) 929-2929; Fax: (802) 864-7626.

Distributed to the U.S. trade and internationally by Penguin Random House Publisher Services.

Berrett-Koehler and the BK logo are registered trademarks of Berrett-Koehler Publishers, Inc.

Printed in Canada

Berrett-Koehler books are printed on long-lasting acid-free paper. When it is available, we choose paper that has been manufactured by environmentally responsible processes. These may include using trees grown in sustainable forests, incorporating recycled paper, minimizing chlorine in bleaching, or recycling the energy produced at the paper mill.

Cataloguing-in-Publication data

Names: Biswas-Diener, Robert, author.
Title: Positive provocation : 25 questions to elevate your coaching
   practice / Robert Biswas-Diener.
Description: First edition. | Oakland, California : Berrett-Koehler
   Publishers, [2023] | Includes bibliographical references and index.
Identifiers: LCCN 2022055229 (print) | LCCN 2022055230 (ebook) | ISBN
   9781523003938 (paperback ; alk. paper) | ISBN 9781523003945 (pdf) | ISBN
   9781523003952 (epub) | ISBN 9781523003969 (audio)
Subjects: LCSH: Personal coaching. | Executive coaching.
Classification: LCC BF637.P36 B562 2023 (print) | LCC BF637.P36 (ebook) |
   DDC 158.3—dc23/eng/20230221
LC record available at https://lccn.loc.gov/2022055229
LC ebook record available at https://lccn.loc.gov/2022055230

First Edition

30 29 28 27 26 25 24 23   10 9 8 7 6 5 4 3 2 1

Interior design: Reider Books
Cover design: Adam Johnson
Copyediting: PeopleSpeak

For my students,
who give me meaning

Contents

Preface

How I Arrived Here

IN 2016, the International Coaching Federation (ICF) invited me to its annual conference—not as a presenter but to fill the role of provocateur. Intended to be an emcee of sorts, the idea of a provocateur is to challenge and engage the audience. The invitation was a dream come true. My entire life, I have been able to see situations from a slightly different angle. What's more, I have not been bashful about challenging the status quo. The ICF's invitation felt like an opportunity to do what I do best.

On Provocation

In preparing for the gig, I gave a fair amount of thought to the concept of provocation. Typical definitions of the word *provoke* have a pretty negative connotation. They suggest that a person is trying to incite, stimulate, or otherwise make someone else uncomfortable, aroused, or angry. My unabridged *Oxford English Dictionary* offers many definitions of provocation, one of which is "calling out to fight." To call a person *provocative* does not seem to be a compliment in the way that calling them *humble* or *generous* does. To many people, provocation is the bridge that internet trolls hide under. This type of provocation is certainly not what I wanted for the ICF audience.

Instead, I relied on my own intuition and relationship with provocation. Regardless of what the dictionary tells us, I view provocation as exciting, interesting, and positive. I think of it as including challenging new ideas, fresh thinking, and a call to reflect on current practices. The examples of provocation that have worked for me in my own life have been new and seemingly contradictory concepts that have forced me to scratch my head: Could Western and Eastern approaches to medicine both be correct? Can a person be humble and confidant simultaneously? Is it possible for a person to be religious even without faith? Over time, I found that these types of questions were the ones that had the greatest gravitational pull for me.

These types of challenging questions, it turns out, are a staple of coaching. Coaches offer their clients challenges large and small not to discount the client but to encourage new thinking. For example, I recently observed a coaching session in which the client was hard on herself. "When I look at other people," she said at one point, "I really value how they take their time to think things through. With myself, however, I never do this. I expect that I should make quick, bold decisions." Without missing a beat, the coach challenged her (softly) by asking, "What would happen if you did value that in yourself?" In this context, challenge was simply the entertainment of alternatives, not a striking down of the client.

As I prepared to challenge the coaches at the ICF conference, positive provocation was born. I found that, to successfully engage with my audience, I would need to challenge without invalidating. There is a big difference between saying, "What you know to be true is wrong" and "What you know to be true is partially correct, but there is nuance you may not yet have considered." It occurred to me that presenting at a meeting can exist along a continuum ranging from statements that are opposed to the audience's current beliefs and knowledge at one end and consistent with those beliefs and knowledge at the other. From a learning perspective, I don't believe that either end of the continuum is all that effective. Dismissing people's beliefs simply leaves them feeling defensive and angry, and they will be closed to learning. Similarly, pandering to their existing knowledge does little to move them forward and may even leave them feeling arrogant in their knowledge. The sweet spot is in the middle: to say things that are new and challenging but still make room for existing beliefs (see figure P.1).

I have come to call this the *90-degree view*. At the risk of me bringing back memories of your high school geometry class, let's review circles: there are 360 degrees in a circle. A 180-degree angle is a flat line and represents opposing line segments. In the social world, this angle is a metaphor for the people who shoot you down, dismiss your ideas, refuse your requests, and hold opposing views. By contrast, the 0-degree angle is your own first-person perspective. You see the world through the 0-degree peephole, with immediate access to all your own memories, values, opinions, and beliefs. Good educators (and coaches) have a sense of where people are and how to push

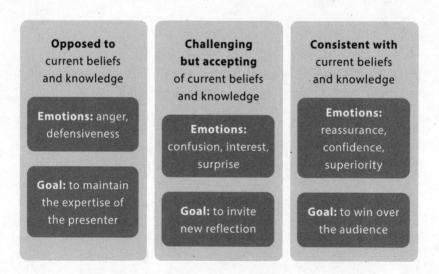

FIGURE P.1. The continuum of challenge in presentations

or pull to engage them in new ways of thinking without completely pulling the rug out from under them: a 90-degree view.

The process of positive provocation is germane not only to my presentation at the ICF conference but also to the coaching endeavor itself. One of my favorite definitions of coaching is "conversations designed to engage the client in self-directed learning." What appeals to me about this stance is that it de-emphasizes goals and emphasizes client learning. When thought of this way, anything that engages client learning would seem to forward the coaching and increase its effectiveness. Offering clients new perspectives, engaging them in reflection about what they know and what they don't, and challenging them to rise to the occasion are all examples of core coaching activities that help clients learn through mild and positive provocation.

Introduction to the Positive Provocation Framework

I WAS ONCE training coaches for the Marcus Buckingham Company. Marcus is a thought leader in the world of strengths psychology, and I admit I was a little nervous to train his staff. These weren't newbies that I could introduce to strengths for the first time. Instead, they were an unusually sophisticated group of people with a huge amount of experience with strengths coaching. I needed to find the knowledge sweet spot to stretch them appropriately. I opened the day with my typical spiel about my 90-degree view and how I wanted to challenge the group without being dismissive. Immediately, a hand shot up. A woman asked, "How can you know what we know to calibrate your challenges effectively?" It was a terrific question.

In fact, her question led me to an insight: effective and positive provocation is not a one-way street. It isn't a matter of me—or any coach or presenter—challenging an audience. Instead, it is one person challenging an audience and, in turn, the audience being open to and accepting that challenge. If I had to write it as a formula, I would note that "positive provocation = (novelty of argument + strength of argument) × openness to argument" (see figure I.1).

On the coach's side of the equation is the "argument," or challenge, if you prefer. The coach makes an educated guess about how novel the challenge will be. For example, I can make a reasonable guess that the statement "Coaches should interrupt clients" will be more challenging than "Coaches should listen to clients." The coach is also called on to make a strong case for the provocation. Using the same example, it is stronger to say, "Strategic interruptions can ensure that incredible moments do not pass by" than "Interrupting is good." The trick, then, for a presenter or a coach is to have considered existing knowledge and to be able to articulate a well-reasoned argument why the existing knowledge is more nuanced than might first be assumed.

The other part of the equation belongs to the client or audience and their open-mindedness and willingness to be changed by the new material. That is, the person has to feel safe enough, be ready enough for growth, and feel resourceful enough to consider the

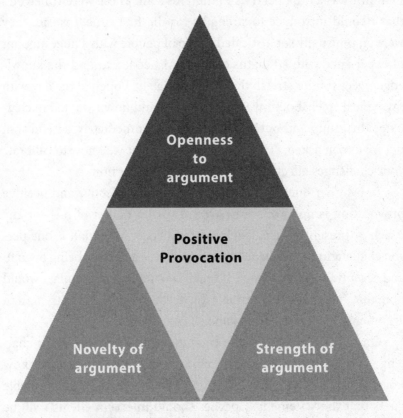

FIGURE I.1. The positive provocation model

challenge. The Sanskrit term *Adhikari-bheda*, found in Hindu scriptures, essentially refers to the idea that a particular person is qualified and ready to receive a teaching. Krishna gives Arjun the teachings of the Bhagavad Gita, for instance, because the latter is uniquely open and ready to receive them at that particular moment. If anything, this reinforces the notion that great coaching is built on creating a relationship that feels safe for the client—not safe *from* challenge but safe enough *to be* challenged.

This Book Is a Positive Provocation

Early on in my coaching career, I scratched my head at a number of standard practices and puzzled over some of the coaching "facts" that I had been taught. Perhaps my devil's-advocate personality was at play, but some things I heard simply did not seem correct. For example, I often heard people distinguish coaching from psychotherapy with the pithy little phrase "Coaching is about the future, and therapy is about the past." This never made any sense to me because it does not withstand even a few seconds of scrutiny. In coaching, we often ask about the past. For instance, we might ask, "When did you successfully navigate a similar problem in the past?" and "When wasn't this a problem?" and "What did you learn from that?" By contrast, skilled therapists often ask about the future. For example, they might ask, "How hopeful are you?" or "What is one thing you look forward to?" or "What's the smallest thing you might be willing to try?" I was never convinced by the past-future distinction and am surprised by how enduring it is.

In my own experience, simply thinking through the adage "Psychotherapy is about the past, and coaching is about the future" was helpful. It wasn't about me dismissing it or thinking I knew better than everyone else. It was about me puzzling out why I had a problem with it and where the argument fell apart and improving it. Once

I rejected the basic past-future premise, I felt called on to offer an alternative. I had to ask myself, "If a focus on the past or future is not an important distinguishing characteristic, then what is?" Finding an answer was tough work because so many aspects of therapy and coaching are similar. Both are conversational technologies, require empathy, rest on the quality of the professional relationship, employ confidentiality, and address client problems and hope for client growth. In the end, the biggest distinction I could identify is that psychotherapy addresses clinically significant distress, and coaching never should. This might not be a perfect argument, but I believe it is superior to the adage I had thrown away.

From that early time in my career, I made it a habit to reconsider standard coaching practices and common wisdom. Even if, in the process of doing so, I wound up accepting them. In fact, I believe that this aspect of provocation is important and often overlooked: challenge is not about rejecting things but about considering things. That is exactly my hope for this book. I want to offer provocative theses that invite you to pause and reflect on your own assumptions about coaching, your own style, and your own preferences. I have seen firsthand how effective this strategy can be with the coaches I train at my own company, Positive Acorn. Rather than teaching them immutable rules, I aim to pull back the curtain to reveal general wisdom that contains both nuance and exceptions. The result, I hope, is emerging coaches who are flexible and reflective.

To be clear, I am not interested in dismissing you, invalidating your beliefs, making you feel defensive, or coming across as superior in any way. I want my provocation to be positive. I want you to lean forward and wonder what I mean, to question how I arrived at my conclusions, and to learn from research on these topics. In each case, I will try to present the most cogent arguments possible. That said, I make no demands that you agree with my way of thinking. You have every right to your own values, experiences, and opinions.

I only offer the idea that, in considering the provocations in this book—regardless of whether you change your mind or if they simply reinforce your current beliefs—you will be better for having gone through the process of reflection.

In this way, this book is intended to mirror the coaching process itself. Coaching is a process that invites clients to reflect on the ways they view themselves and their current situation and to articulate a desirable future. *Positive Provocation* offers the same invitation to you. At its core, it asks questions such as "What as coaches should we be doing?"

As an example, it makes sense, with the previous sentence in mind, to mention a statement I commonly hear in the world of coaching: "I don't believe in *shoulds*." In essence, people who espouse this sentiment recognize that sometimes clients act out of some artificial or irrelevant sense of obligation. Fair enough. On the other hand, *shoulds* are pretty important. Most of the cultures in the world place a heavy premium on personal duty and obligation. For example, they believe that friends should be loyal, that people should take care of their sick family members, that we should help strangers in distress, and that we should use our talents rather than squander them. Each of these is a moral statement that guides desirable behavior. Shoulds not only define how to live life well but also bear on how to coach well: we should be present, we should have a positive view of our clients, we should listen carefully, and so on. Who created these obligations? More importantly, are all of these assumed coaching duties correct or useful? Should we give advice from time to time? Should we engage clients in addressing their self-limiting beliefs? Should we always use the client's language rather than offering our own? Should we trust aha moments? These prompts are exactly the types of provocations that will be discussed in this book.

Whether we call great coaching a *challenge*, or *positive provocation*, or the more saccharine *invitation to reflect*, it involves pushing on some fundamental assumptions and behaviors. If we employ this technique in the service of our clients, why not on ourselves as well? Shouldn't we coaches also be asking ourselves questions that are equally powerful in their seismic capacity? The trick, of course, is that it is exceedingly difficult to do so. In fact, to offer questions that our clients have not thought of for themselves is our fundamental purpose as coaches. In the same way, we cannot easily shift our own thinking with our own thinking. That is the purpose of this book: to consider each of my provocations as if they were a coaching question that you are free to answer in any way you see fit. In fact, you will notice that many of the chapter titles in this book are questions.

How to Use This Book

EVERY READER is unique. You will all differ in terms of personality, communication style, and openness to new ideas, to name just three ways in which you are distinct from one another. This means that each of you will have your own unique experience of this book. Some of you will find my language too challenging, and others will perceive it as playful and stimulating. One major difference in readers will be their years of professional experience. If we can divide coaches roughly into beginner, intermediate, and advanced practitioners, members of each of these three groups will have distinct reactions to the provocations found herein. Theoretically, beginners ought to find the material fairly challenging because it will fly in the face of some of the common tropes in coaching. More seasoned coaches, on the other hand, will likely have arrived at some of these challenges on their own and find some to be less provocative. It is my hope that, across the chapters of this book, everyone will find at least a few ideas that spark reflection, invite inquiry, and offer the possibility of deepening beliefs and improving practice.

If we understand provocation to mean "shocking" or "challenging," then we can assume that the provocations in this book will diminish in some abstract scale of intensity (the y axis in figure H.1) along the continuum of coaching experience (the x axis in figure H.1). I would argue that shock value is not the best metric for this reflective practice. Instead, we should think of positive provocation as being successful to

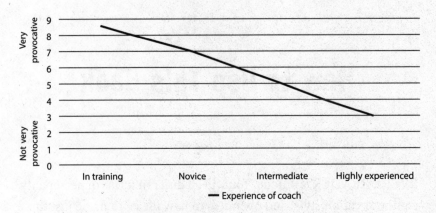

FIGURE H.1. How provocative is this book?

the extent that it presents ideas that feel worth considering, in a way that helps people remain open-minded, and invites reflection that has the potential to improve practice.

Here's one example of a provocation for coaches just starting out: Many novice coaches are interested in the business development side of coaching. They want to build a client roster, establish a business footprint, and develop a website. One common practice adopted by coaches in the early stages of their career is to sell packages of coaching services. That is, they ask clients to contract and pay for a set number of sessions, often offering a small discount for doing so. I cannot remember if I was ever explicitly told to do this, but I know I absorbed it through osmosis by seeing that all the coaches around me were doing this. The rationale for this practice typically falls into two parts:

- By getting clients to commit to multiple sessions, the coach invests them in the coaching process itself.
- By securing multiple sessions, the coach has some job security and can, therefore feel comfortable in passing some discount back to the client.

Admittedly, when I first hung out my shingle as a coach, I adopted this approach. Like many of my colleagues, I offered packages of four sessions at a slightly discounted price. After only a few months in the business, however, I began to question this practice. If coaching is supposed to be co-created, I wondered, why am I making a unilateral decision about what my client needs? Wouldn't you think it was strange if you went to a dentist who said, "You must prepay for six cleanings because that is the best way to get you invested in your own hygiene" or if you hired a guitar teacher who told you, "You must pay for and commit to twenty lessons because, let's be honest, no one is learning to play the guitar in just six sessions"? I began to wonder where the client's voice was in this common practice. As a result, I changed my policy. I began asking my clients, "What makes sense for you?" We discussed our best guesses of how long our working engagement might be, and I made more room for clients to pay me in a way that made sense to them. Some paid for multiple sessions, while others paid for one at a time. Some paid before, and others paid after.

In the end, I am not flatly opposed to selling packages of coaching. I am, however, opposed to doing so simply because it is common practice. I want novice coaches to reflect on their reasons for offering packages, to consider the ways that it might be changed to better include the needs and voice of the client, and to be more flexible in their approach.

Intermediate coaches, by contrast, are less concerned about business development than they are about good practices. They tend to be in a period of growth and are interested in developing their coaching skills so they can serve their clients better. A positive provocation that might land better with this group is to question any assumptions about what actually happens in a coaching session. To this end, I found a recent piece of research by Jim Gavin and his colleagues to be illuminating.[1] They were able to carefully observe three coaching sessions of forty-five different coaches and parse what is normally hidden behind the veil of confidentiality. What did they find?

- In the thirty-seven minutes—the average length of a session—coaches made fifty utterances. Half of these were "minimal encouragers," such as "mm-hmm," "I see," or "huh."
- Of the remaining twenty-five times that coaches spoke, 66 percent of their remarks were questions or attempts to influence client perspective (such as through reframing).
- Of the questions coaches asked, only one-tenth of 1 percent were about the client's "ecosystem."
- Of the attempts to influence, 12 percent were direct instruction, such as giving advice or offering direction.
- Of their total remarks, 20 percent represented "listening" in the form of clarifying, summarizing, or repeating client words.
- The remaining handful of expressions were counted as miscellaneous.

Being confronted with the results of this type of research can provoke professional development. We all make assumptions about what happens in our own coaching sessions, and it is easy to forget how biased our mental ledgers can be. When I read the statistics from this study, I immediately assumed that I am using far more minimal encouragers than I might be aware of. This probably isn't a fatal flaw for the coaching relationship and might even be occasionally beneficial. Even so, my instinct was to start paying more attention to and reducing these in my coaching. The results were also a call to action to inquire about the client's setting more, to reduce the amount of summarization I likely do, and to reduce the amount of instruction or advice I give (actually, for me, this amount is far less than the 12 percent identified in this research, so I won't have to make a big change there).

In many ways, *Positive Provocation*'s ideal audience is intermediate coaches. By calling many common coaching practices into question—such as interrupting, making assumptions about clients, or using the client's language—coaches with two to twelve years of experience can reconnect with and improve the very foundations of their practice.

Something for more advanced coaches can also be found between the covers of this book—perhaps especially so. I have experienced this firsthand in my conversations with Christian van Nieuwerburgh. Christian is a coach with years of experience and is the executive director of Growth Coaching International. He has also helped to set up graduate programs in coaching psychology at universities in England and Ireland. Christian is a terrific thinker about all matters coaching, has unique cultural insights, and has examples from years of experience to back up his claims. During the COVID-19 pandemic, Christian and I spoke on an almost weekly basis. Our conversations had no formal aim, and they often meandered and backtracked. More than anything, we challenged one another to think about coaching in new ways. These provocations often came in the form of questions—just like good coaching—to which neither of us could quickly or easily articulate an answer. Here are some examples:

- Do coaches have an obligation to model healthy living and well-being practices?
- Should coaches refuse certain clients based on their own personal values, or do we have some duty to put our values in the metaphorical back seat and offer our best services to all?
- Do coaches have agendas of their own?
- If coaches intuitively used positive psychology approaches but had never heard of or read about the science of positive psychology, would they be "doing" positive psychology

coaching (that is, is familiarity with the science a prerequisite to practice)?

- To what extent do coaches engage in diagnosis?
- What are the perils of using humor in coaching?

Behind these questions are provocative theses: that humor can be potentially harmful in coaching, that clients are observing coaches and learning from them, that the qualifications for various types of coaching are not well articulated. The list goes on. In my conversations with Christian, we placed less emphasis on arriving at *the* answer than we did at thinking through *an* answer to advance our understanding of the basic clockworks of coaching. It is my hope that this same process will appeal to highly seasoned coaches as they consider the positive provocations in this book.

Your Positive Provocation Plan

Positive Provocation is not a book that is meant to be read from cover to cover and certainly not in a single sitting. Like vitamins, physical exercise, and travel, challenges are not useful if they are consumed by binging. Instead, they need to be paid out over time. There needs to be space to consider them and accommodate their various lessons. Unlike your favorite beach read, this book is not and should not be a page-turner. Instead, this book is more like a terrific meal that should be consumed gradually over several courses and a significant length of time and punctuated with conversation in between. To be clear, if you try to read this book straight through, your eyes will blur, the text might feel repetitive or preachy, and the luster of each provocation will dim.

To make this idea clearer and more formal, you can think of there being a *Positive Provocation* framework. It consists of the recommended steps to get the most out of these coaching reflections.

The Provocation Itself

In the first step, you read each chapter. They tend to be only a few pages long. Let the ideas in each provocation simmer. Notice any feelings or reactions that arise in you. Pay attention to how similar or different the thesis of a provocation is to how you already think about coaching. See what additional examples or counterexamples you can create. Discuss the idea with other coaches.

My task in creating these provocations is to offer ideas about common coaching practices and beliefs. That said, I want to be clear that I do not want *Positive Provocation* to be a collection of my own opinions. We all have opinions, and why should mine be more meritorious than yours? In creating each provocation, I tried to include real-world case studies, ideas from other thought leaders in the field, theories and results from science, and other elements that can elevate this book from a trollish diatribe to a thoughtful collection of arguments.

The Experimental Phase

During this step you test the ideas contained in each positive provocation, not as a thought experiment but in a practical way in your own coaching sessions. Consider in what practical ways the thesis might be applied to coaching. Whether the provocation is wholly true, partially true, or false, what would it mean for your coaching practice? This exploration is especially important in instances in which the challenge might improve practice, such as when coaches recognize and manage their own private agendas or when they are more likely to incorporate the client's voice while considering the number of sessions they offer. Applying new knowledge and seeing how it manifests in coaching can take learning to a deeper level.

I recently heard an example of this phenomenon from a novice coach whom I trained. She said, "For months, you have been telling us that clients have their own insights and expertise, and that—all too often—they have their own answers within them." She went on to say that while she understood the message at a theoretical level, it never felt tangible. Then, she started coaching more. She logged fifty hours of client contact, and she started trusting her clients to come up with their own solutions. She started asking more questions and avoided the temptation to give advice or be directive. She told me, "It was a major change for me. I finally really believed what you had taught us, believed it deep down because I finally experienced it in my own practice."

The Incorporation Phase

During the incorporation phase, you figure out how—if at all—you will integrate the new way of thinking or doing into your coaching practice.

More than anything, I want for you, the reader, to give this a try. I ask that you consider each positive provocation, even if you ultimately reject it. I hope that by thinking it through and—more importantly—testing the ideas in your own coaching practice, you will end up being a better coach, one who has a richer understanding of the coaching process, is more articulate about your own beliefs, and feels more engaged with the craft because this process has breathed new life into it for you.

Here are my specific recommendations for using this book. I have created twenty-five positive provocations for you to consider. That number is no accident. I envision this book as a course of reflections with which you could interact over an entire calendar year. That would mean that each provocation is two weeks' worth of consideration.

The first week, you would read the material, think about it, and have conversations with others about it. The second week, you would try it out in your own coaching and see what emerges. You would then be ready to incorporate it—to the extent you will—and move on to the next provocation. I believe that this method, if followed even loosely, will pay out the information slowly enough to give you ample opportunity to learn it and to consolidate that learning.

Finally, I have organized the provocations thematically:

- Part one deals with the *fundamental philosophies* of coaching, such as it being a nondirective relationship.
- Part two focuses on provocations related to *how we communicate* as coaches, such as discouraging interruptions.
- Part three shifts to *coaching concepts* that emerge in sessions, such as aha moments.
- Part four focuses on *coaching interventions*, such as challenging self-limiting beliefs.
- Part five is a single provocation: my argument that coaching should be *informed by science.*

Although the provocations are laid out from the most foundational (fundamental philosophies) to the most practical (coaching interventions) you can read them in any order you see fit. Each is written in a stand-alone fashion and can be read in any order you see fit. You may find benefit from jumping between the sections so you are reflecting on many different aspects of coaching. Or it might be just as helpful to read them in the order they are presented here, building from the ground up. I'm not sure which strategy is superior, but I will definitely reflect on my assumptions about each.

Enjoy!

PART ONE
Philosophies of Coaching

ALTHOUGH coaching is international and diverse in its practice, some fundamental philosophies can be found in coach training and practice around the globe. For example, most coaches seem to hold the view that clients have the potential to figure out their own problems. That is, clients are well positioned to understand what they know and don't know, who could help them, what resources are available to them, and how to form a plan that makes sense in their own context. This and similar beliefs are so foundational to what we do that they rarely get questioned.

This part questions these philosophical understandings of coaching and provides a discussion of foundational issues upon which effective coaching is built, such as ethical practice and an understanding of adult learning theories. It begins with the question, Why is it so hard to be a great coach? This seems like a natural starting point since this book is aimed at elevating coaching practice. Indeed, the world is full of good coaches, and perhaps being a good coach is good enough. Making the jump from novice to good appears much easier than making the jump from good to great. This provocation explores these ideas, although it is up to you to decide the degree to which you accept them.

The other provocations in this part address equally foundational tenets of coaching: that it is nondirective, that coaches don't (or shouldn't) have agendas of their own, that coaching solves problems, that ethics should be less boring, and that coaching is originally about training. This part invites you to reflect on your own deeply held convictions and assumptions about coaching and how it works.

Why Is It So Hard to Be a Great Coach?

TRUE CONFESSION: I like to be challenged by thoughtful provocations. When I come across a counterintuitive, fresh, and well-reasoned idea, I get excited by it, even if I don't agree with it. One of the coaches who has consistently challenged me is David Peterson. In my conversations with David, who was director of leadership and coaching at Google for a decade, he has consistently shown a penchant for thinking outside the box. I have heard him refute a number of coaching's sacred cows: coaches do have their own agendas, coaches can ask closed-ended questions, and coaches can occasionally give advice. His ideas are provocative and, in my opinion, exactly what coaching needs to improve.

David once wrote that it is easy to become a good coach, and just as easy to remain a good coach, but difficult to be a great coach.[1] That rings true. I watch a lot of coaching demonstrations and have as many conversations about coaching as I can. I've seen scores of people with good social skills, empathy, and verbal intelligence learn to coach well. I have seen fewer coaches shine in a way that makes my jaw drop in envy and awe. Learning to be a good coach is largely a matter of honing a few relatively straightforward skills and then

3

adding one's own natural social and emotional intelligence. All too often, however, people get stuck at that level. They plateau at good without ever getting promoted to great.

This might not be a problem. Not everyone can be above average, and a world full of good coaches is a nice thought. Even so, I think it makes sense to at least consider greatness. To begin, let's consider what that might even mean. Professional proficiency can be understood through several frameworks, and I will offer versions of them here:

Novices—Novices are new to the field and just learning the basic philosophies, frameworks, and skills of coaching. They often struggle with counterintuitive ideas, such as the prohibition against giving advice.

Advanced beginners—These people are near the end of their training. They have a conceptual understanding of coaching and can execute basic coaching skills. They are not particularly adept, however, at dealing with complicated scenarios. They also have a tendency to focus on problem-solving rather than coaching the person in a more general way.

Competent professionals—These people can pass a certification exam, have a professional mindset, and deliver satisfactory services for a wide range of clients.

Proficient performers—These people are good coaches. They are flexible, are eager to develop, and can handle a wide range of complicated scenarios. They are helpful to their clients and can use advanced skills and take appropriate risks.

Great coaches—I am avoiding the word *master* here because I have seen some coaches with a master certification who do not seem all that masterful. I am not referring to a specific professional credential but rather to a person's actual ability. Great coaches engage in deep reflective practice, can handle complicated situations, innovate new techniques, notice critical coaching moments, have accurate self-knowledge, and have developed excellent professional intuition. That is, they make great choices about which directions might be most fruitful and about which techniques to use and in which moments.

I would be happy if the world of coaching was full of proficient performers and great coaches. I also understand that most people have to pass through the earlier stages to achieve this level of performance. I worry, however, that too many coaches who are competent professionals think that they are great coaches. There are several common—and solvable—barriers to coaching greatness.

Coaching Culture

I am going to expose myself to potential criticism here when I suggest that coaching culture itself acts as an impediment to great coaching. The people who self-select into the profession are drawn from all walks of life. Even so, some common qualities unite us and give rise to a global coaching culture. First, coaches generally have a service mentality. We enjoy helping others. Second, we tend to be positive and upbeat people. We are optimistic about the prospects for change. Third, we tend to have an entrepreneurial mindset. We don't mind setting up our own businesses. Taken together, you get a culture that is upbeat about helping clients and selling those services.

In my experience, our professional culture leads too often to forms of inauthenticity. I frequently hear coaches boast about their "bestselling book," the unnamed high-profile executives with whom they have worked, or how helpful they have been to their clients. It boils down to rampant self-promotion. Often, these statements are exaggerations and, more often, are cherry-picked from the coach's entire experience. I have never once heard a coach say, "The best thing I ever did as a coach was to take six months off when I started to burn out" or "I glance at my text messages sometimes when I am coaching, but I wish I wouldn't because it is a terrible thing to do" or "I worked with a client for three sessions, and I just could not help them, and we parted ways" or "My book was a bestseller in a subcategory of Amazon, but sold only one thousand copies total." In essence, coaching culture itself subtly reinforces an inflationary sense of self, even while it endorses humility.

The master coaches I know seldom talk about their accomplishments, especially publicly. Instead, they are more likely to talk about their own learning, the new ideas they are playing with, or a new approach that challenges their accepted wisdom. They are more likely to own up to their mistakes and admit to not knowing. They are actively and effortfully focusing more on their improvements than their self-promotion.

Mindset

Many readers will be familiar with my colleague Carol Dweck and her research on growth and fixed mindsets.[2] In essence, people with a growth mindset are more open to learning from mistakes, persevering, and embracing challenges. By contrast, those with a fixed mindset avoid challenges, give up more easily, are more immune to feedback, and tend to be more threatened by the success of other people. Unfortunately, people who learn about this research often have a simplistic takeaway: the growth mindset is the good one, and the fixed mindset is the bad one. They assume that we should all just have a growth mindset. In fact, this universal growth mindset fits with a coaching philosophy that anyone can improve at anything.

When I teach about research on mindset, I ask my students, "Five years from now, will you be better, worse, or the same in your ability to drive a car?" Most people (but not all) say that they will be better. Almost no one says worse. I believe this sheds light on common assumptions about the process of improvement. Most of us—and I am as vulnerable to this as anyone—assume that we will get better at a skill simply by doing it over and over. If I drive each day for the next five years, how could I not improve? I'll tell you how! Over the next five years, my reaction time will slow, as will my ability to quickly process multiple streams of information. At best, any gains in experience will be a wash with these declines.

I further challenge my students with the following question: "What are you doing to become a better driver?" That brings most people up short. Driving to work and to the store over and over with no variation or conscious thought does not seem like a reliable way to improve one's driving skills. If you wanted to actively improve your driving, you would take a class, such as one on driving in snow; you would have to get ongoing feedback on your driving; and you would have to identify the specific elements of your driving that you are trying to improve. In sum, you would gain the most if you set specific development goals and then systematically pursued them.

Conclusion

Improvement toward greatness in coaching has to be more than fulfilling continuing education credit requirements and coaching on a regular basis. Those steps are terrific ways to maintain your current good practice, like getting regular oil changes to maintain your car. To really catapult forward, however, you need to invest more effort. You need to be challenged, get feedback, and see change. Can you, for example, identify practices that you have ditched as you have gained more professional sophistication? Are there coaching practices you used in the past but no longer believe are helpful? Have you modified techniques to improve them? Do you receive peer or other forms of supervision? Do you experiment with your own coaching approaches? Do you engage with people who coach differently than you do to learn from them or argue with them? Do you keep a journal of insights into your own coaching and lessons you have learned about the coaching process? As these questions suggest, coaching development takes intentional effort. When this intentional effort is paired with years of experience, the door to coaching greatness is unlocked.

REFLECT AND EXPERIMENT

- Looking back on the past year, how are you a better coach than you were a year ago? How are you defining *better*? Be as specific as possible.
- What, specifically, are you doing to increase the quality of your coaching? What have you added, improved upon, or given up to make you a better coach? How will you know the extent to which this has been successful?
- Consider discussing improvement with other coaches. What is it they are doing? What themes, techniques, or concepts do they focus on? How do they go about the business of intentional improvement?

Is Coaching Nondirective?

SEVERAL YEARS ago, I had the great fortune of visiting the Topkapı Palace in Istanbul. It is a sprawling sixteenth-century Ottoman palace with commanding views of the Bosporus, the Maiden's Tower lighthouse, and the Karaköy district. The palace also includes an audio tour. I meandered from the harem to a mosque, from a garden to a dormitory. All the while, a recorded voice explained the history, customs, decorations, and politics of the sultans. I struggle to turn off the coach part of my brain, though, and the experience provoked a little wonder: Was the tour directive or nondirective? On the one hand, the tour encouraged me to walk the grounds in a prescribed order; on the other hand, I was free to linger in certain areas or skip others entirely.

When we speak about the degree to which coaching might or might not be directive, what exactly are we talking about? As the words suggest, directive approaches are more controlling and more pointed and involve the coach more. By contrast, nondirective approaches are more broad and less controlling and emphasize the client. See table 2.1 for a theoretical distinction between the two approaches.

TABLE 2.1. Distinction between directive and nondirective support

Directive responding and support	Nondirective responding and support
Involves an agenda the coach has	Is centered on the client's agenda
Focuses on prescriptions	Focuses on options
Attempts to influence specific actions or thoughts	Invites reflection about possible actions or thoughts
Assumes more responsibility is on the coach for action	Assumes more responsibility is on the client for action

To see how these two approaches play out in everyday life, researcher Diana Stewart and her colleagues examined support offered by people interested in improving healthy habits (specifically, eating vegetables, reducing alcohol intake, and being physically active).[1] These subjects were not coaches, nor were they the stereotypical college student sample. They were 304 adult community members ranging in age from forty to seventy years, who represented diverse ethnicities and marital statuses. The research team used statistical analyses to classify each specific supportive overture. Telling a person what to eat, for example, fell into the directive category, while showing interest landed in the nondirective camp. Pointing out how certain views are harmful or foolish was directive. Asking about how a person was doing was nondirective. Importantly, the research team found that the nondirective support was associated with gains in each of the three areas of health while directive support was not.

This research reinforces the intuitive appeal of nondirective approaches. The results are a tip of the hat to the kind of empowerment, respect, and acceptance that coaches thread into each session, which must be why there seems to be such widespread agreement about this issue in coaching.

What Coaching Thought Leaders Say

The question of directiveness in coaching would appear to be an issue that had been laid to rest years ago. Everyone seems to agree: coaching is nondirective. Or, at the very least, coaching should be nondirective. You hear this sentiment expressed in basic coach training, espoused at coaching conferences, and written about in the coaching literature. There is widespread agreement that nondirectiveness is a fundamental element of coaching, and one that distinguishes it from other disciplines.

Thought leaders in coaching triangulate this view:

- Michael Bungay Stanier thinks being directive makes people overdependent.[2]
- John Whitmore believes coaches can effectively act as detached awareness-raisers.[3]
- Christian van Nieuwerburgh says the core skills of coaching are listening, noticing, asking questions, and summarizing.[4]
- Laura Whitworth and colleagues argue that the agenda does not come from the coach but the client.[5]
- Marcia Reynolds believes providing expert advice isn't coaching.[6]
- Mary Beth O'Neill suggests that directiveness is more important when competence is low and support is more important when motivation is low.[7]
- Graham Alexander and Ben Renshaw believe the most effective coaches help their clients discover their own ways of moving forward.[8]

The examples go on. In each case, the thought leaders in our field identify nondirectiveness as the secret sauce that makes coaching special.

What's more, their sentiments appear to be supported by research. In one study, researchers Tina Salter and Judie Gannon aimed to distinguish the professional approaches of executive coaches, coaching psychologists, sports coaches, and mentors.[9] To do so, they interviewed eighteen professionals, each representing one of these categories. The researchers found that mentors and sports coaches were more directive, while executive coaches and coaching psychologists were less directive. This dovetails with research by Anna Dolot, who used 100 participants to chart the frequency of nondirective communication techniques in coaching.[10] The most frequent techniques reported were building a relationship (89 percent of respondents), active listening (85 percent), and asking questions (81 percent).

I think we can agree that, as a rule, coaches should not give advice or hijack the client's agenda and replace it with one of their own—if, in fact, that is what we mean by directive. My positive provocation here is centered around two distinct questions, both of which ask us to reevaluate core assumptions about coaching. The first is to question whether the distinction between directive and nondirective (presented above) is the whole truth. Is coaching as nondirective as we often make it out to be? The second challenging question is to wonder about the ways in which directedness might potentially be beneficial.

Is Coaching Really as Nondirective as We Make It Out to Be?

One mental image I have always had of coaching is that of a coach and a client walking down a long hallway shoulder to shoulder. On each side of the hall are an infinite number of closed doors. Each time the coach asks a question, they—metaphorically speaking—place a hand on a knob and throw that door open. "Wanna look in here?" they essentially ask. Some rooms are full of valuables, and the coach and client linger in those spaces for a while. Others are dusty affairs without much to offer, and the pair quickly moves on down the hallway. To the extent that this vision of the process of coaching is helpful, it is undeniable that coaches have influence. Let's be honest, we are making decisions about which doors to open. We can tell ourselves that it is all co-created—that clients have the final say in whether they want to enter the room or how long they want to stay there. They do not, however, have any say whatsoever in the rooms we—the coaches—choose to pass by. Clients *react* to coach summaries, statements, observations, and questions. Each time we speak, we *direct* clients to make a choice about that, even while purposefully omitting other topics. If it helps, we can think of direction not as advice but as influence.

What is it we are directing? One short answer is attention. I think most coaches would be comfortable with the idea that coaches are directive insofar as we focus client attention on resources, frames, processes, and other topics that clients might not have already considered. In large part, this is exactly what clients hire us for. They have already taken a first pass at thinking through their problems, goals, and decisions, and now they want us to direct them toward potentially fruitful new avenues of consideration. Sure, they do the considering, but we do the directing.

Among the most vocal advocates of directiveness—broadly understood—in coaching is Ian Day.[11] According to Day, the origins of coaching are to be found, in no small part, in person-centered, nondirective counseling. This has led to many kind people self-selecting into the coaching profession because of its highly supportive nature. I suspect that Day is happy that people are supportive and kind, but he rightly pushes back on this as the foundation of coaching. In fact, he goes so far as to list three common problems with this approach:

- *Collusion*—According to Day, coaches can be so neutral, work so hard to remove themselves from influence, or so strongly believe they cannot possibly make assumptions about their clients that they end up colluding with the clients' perceptions. In essence, they miss opportunities to challenge, stretch, or surprise their clients.
- *Irrelevance*—Day argues that coaches can hold client agendas too inflexibly and thereby miss opportunities to expand from "coaching the problem" (what the client wants) to "coaching the person" (often not explicitly stated as a client agenda but potentially helpful in empowering the client). Here, seasoned coaches recognize that we sometimes have small agendas of our own and that we must carefully reflect on how these crop up and where they might actually be beneficial.
- *Self-obsession*—Coaches can see a wider perspective than clients. Often, clients—by their very human nature—are the stars of their own stories. They can narrowly focus on their own wants, needs, and benefits while overlooking the broader social context in which they live. Here, I would add to Day's critique that coaches can be similarly self-obsessed with our own professional virtue. This is, in part, why I enjoy the inherent messiness in trying to figure out how much of my coaching should be nondirective and in which ways direction is helpful.

Day's answer to the perils of nondirection is what he and his coauthor call "challenging coaching."[12] The antidote to myopic support is challenge, and—in my own opinion—challenge is a form of directedness. In this way, coaches are similar to sports coaches who seek to stretch their athletes by making them train harder and look beyond their positions to see the larger game. In challenging coaching, the idea is not to hijack the client's agenda or give them advice but rather to stretch them while simultaneously believing in their ability to be stretched (see table 2.2). Day suggests that a single coaching session might contain moments when we find ourselves temporarily in any one of these four categories.

TABLE 2.2. Challenge and support in coaching

		Low challenge	High challenge
High support	Title	Classic nondirectiveness	Classic empowerment
	Description	"Coach as cheerleader or supporter"	"Coach as trusting and trusted challenger"
	Emphasis	Listening, understanding, accepting	Shifting the client's perspective, balancing the tension of acceptance and challenge
	Benefit	Validating, encouraging, relationship building	Empowering the client, supporting client growth, trusting client's ability to withstand challenge
Low support	Title	Classic apathy	Classic directiveness
	Description	"Coach as dispassionate facilitator"	"Coach as devil's advocate or mentor"
	Emphasis	Detaching from the person or process, choosing not to explore a particular theme	Emphasizing advice, giving critical feedback, challenging, pointing out limits of current methods or performance
	Benefit	Remaining detached from the client's problem or story	Accelerating learning when it works

Conclusion

In a 2011 study, Diana Stewart and her colleagues examined directive and nondirective approaches to supporting people in a twelve-
week weight-loss program.[13] In the directive condition, participants
received direct advice about diet and exercise, a short-term goal
plan, and direct feedback and encouragement regarding progress.
In the nondirective condition, participants were supplied with general information, given the opportunity to create their own goals,
and provided with basic encouragement and feedback. The majority
of the participants lost weight during the program, and—in many
cases—directive support was especially beneficial. This single study
has methodological limitations and shouldn't be taken as the final
word that directive support is the best way to support clients. You
and I can both make strong cases for the ways in which a twelve-
week diet program is distinct from the coaching we do. Rather, the
author's discussion provides interesting food for thought.

The Stewart research team suggests that more directive support
might be particularly appropriate to instances in which clients meet
one or more of the following criteria: (1) are ready to take action,
(2) lack critical skills or knowledge, or (3) they are stuck in an unde-
sirable pattern of thinking or behavior. By contrast, nondirective
approaches might be particularly useful when clients are contemplating or preparing for change or when they need support to maintain
change. In this way, the Stewart research team echoes the sentiments
of Ian Day—namely, that we might be limiting ourselves when we say
that coaching is only one way, such as the idea that it is and should
be only nondirective.

In expanding our understanding of coaching, we can play with
the idea that the coaching relationship might be more flexible than
we assume. During certain sessions, or certain moments of sessions,
we might vary slightly in how directive we are with the idea that we

still lean toward a general nondirectiveness. What's more, we can expand our notions of directing to think of it more as influencing, as in the case of directing client attention, challenging assumptions, reframing perceptions, or not getting pulled into the gravitational pull of the client's problems.

REFLECT AND EXPERIMENT

- What is your own definition of *directive*? Can you place various professional roles on a continuum of more or less directive, as you understand the term?
- Consider your own experiences with directive professional interactions. What did you find helpful about nondirective support? What were the limitations of nondirective support? What about the potential benefits and limitations of directive support?
- Think about your own coaching. In what ways do you influence the coaching process? What types of influence would you prefer to avoid?
- Try overtly directing the conversation within the bounds of the stated agenda. What happens?
- How much direction do your clients want? Have you ever asked them?

What If Coaches Had Agendas?

IT IS OFTEN said that coaches do not have agendas. I believe this sentiment means that the client directs the agenda for the session, not the coach. This makes sense because it provides some protection from coaches who might otherwise hijack the agenda and go in directions that are not central to the client's wishes. I have occasionally witnessed when this happens. A coach desperately wants for a client to accept herself, or a coach pressures a client to quit putting so much pressure on himself, or a coach tries to reassure a client. Each of these approaches is well-intentioned and comes from what the coach wants, as opposed to what the client is explicitly asking for or trying to accomplish.

Yet, what if these coach-centric goals are occasionally useful? What if, from time to time, it is not only acceptable but beneficial for coaches to have agendas of their own? To explore this idea more, you could engage in a technique common to speech and debate clubs: arguing the other side. Pretend you are charged with a mandate to argue in favor of coaches having agendas. Do your best to make your case: list the types of coach agendas that might be beneficial and offer a rationale for your argument. Try to imagine specific instances in which a coach's agenda might be appropriate.

Four Types of Coach Agendas

To aid you in this process, consider the following four types of coach-centric agendas.

The Agenda for the Overall Coaching Relationship

It is not uncommon for coaches to focus on a niche area. In life coaching, you find coaches focusing on self-compassion or mindfulness. In career coaching, you find strengths-based coaches. In executive coaching, practitioners focus heavily on leadership competencies, such as strategic thinking and agility. In each of these cases, coaches are brazenly declaring their own passion for and endorsement of a particular goal. They are, in essence, saying, "Work with me, and you will become more self-compassionate, more plugged into your own strengths, or a more strategic thinker." In our profession, we tend to accept this level of coaching agenda because it ticks the box for a "co-created relationship." That is, the coach is up front about these leanings in the initial session with a client, and the client has the opportunity to say, "Yeah, I value that" or "No, I would prefer not to work with you."

This is clear in my own practice. Whether I am coaching someone around a career change, about work-life balance, or through a newly promoted leadership role, I address the topic of well-being. I state this at the outset. Specifically, I tell my prospective clients that well-being is an important aspect of coaching. Personally, I do not coach "goals at any cost" and certainly not at the cost of well-being. In essence, I get client agreement to ask about well-being, even in the context of client goals that are not primarily well-being related, such as giving feedback or succession planning.

The Agenda for the Coaching Process

In coaching, both parties are generally comfortable with the idea that the coach takes some ownership of the facilitative process. Perhaps this is the reason why we don't bat an eye when a coach says, "I am a solutions-focused practitioner." If we held the most stringent view of a co-created relationship, we would—in this instance—argue that coaches should ask their clients the degree to which they want to pursue a solutions-focused approach. We do not do this, however. We simply assume that it is fine for coaches to adopt a way of coaching. You can see this threaded deeply into the very fabric of coaching itself: many coaches challenge so-called self-limiting beliefs under the tacit assumption that doing so is a benefit to the client. To some degree, this represents the coach's worldview and not the client's.

The Agenda That Occurs in the Moment

We all know that the agenda for a session can evolve over the course of the session as new insights emerge. Most of us have been trained to address such shifts with our clients. When we notice the session veering from the original goal, we comment on it and inquire with our clients about their desire to shift or stay the course. Emergent agendas are perhaps the most challenging to the notion that coaches don't have agendas. This is because, at times, what emerges is an insight in the coach. A coach might suddenly see something that the client does not. Perhaps the coach comments on it, in the form of a summary, such as "It occurs to me suddenly that there are really two versions of yourself you are talking about here: your past self and your current self." At our best, we simply offer such statements to clients to see what kind of traction they might garner or how clients might react. Even so, the client will likely shift into this way of thinking if the coach's observation has even a seed of truth. What follows is a discussion that aims to find great alignment between these two selves. The truth is, aligning two selves—in this example—is the product of the coach's thinking. All of us have done this from time to time, perhaps not even being aware of it. And, often, it *is* helpful to the client.

The Agenda for Ourselves

Coaches love to say how humble they are, how little expertise they have, and what a beginner's mind they are able to achieve. It is as if the world of coaching is full of Buddhas who have successfully transcended self-interest and easily check their egos at the door once the coaching session starts. I'm not there yet. I still find that I harbor my own personal agendas—I want to be a competent coach, I want to be an ethical coach, and I want to see the best in my clients. I admit, I primarily want these things because I think they lead to better service. That is, I largely aim for these goals in the service of my clients. I have to ask myself, though, if these objectives are 100 percent in the service of my clients, or if feeling competent is also just a fundamental psychological need, if having integrity helps me like myself more, and if seeing the best in my clients just makes my job easier. I don't have the magic solution to parsing how much of our desires are ego based and how much are in the service of our clients. I do believe, however, that the claim that they are wholly about our clients feels disingenuous to me, although the aspiration is laudable.

Conclusion

In the end, I think we can push past the idea that coaches have no agendas whatsoever. Instead, we ought to be asking the following:

What types of agendas do coaches have? Which of these agendas tend to be helpful and which are more likely harmful to our clients and to the coaching process?

REFLECT AND EXPERIMENT

- Make two lists: one that represents everything you want for your client and one that represents everything you want for your coaching. Where is there overlap, and which elements are clearly distinct?
- Define what coaching success means for you. To what extent is your notion of success entirely about your client?
- Try setting an intentional agenda before a session. Maybe it's "I will check in more with my client about the process" or "I will completely own my agenda of wanting the client to be more self-accepting." See how it feels to enter and experience coaching with an explicit personal agenda.
- Pay particularly close attention to your reactions when your clients experience either setbacks or successes. To what degree do you take some personal ownership of wins and losses?
- Try making a list of coach agendas that you would find acceptable and those you would not. What distinguishes the two lists?

Are We Solving Problems or Improving?

THERE IS a mismatch in coaching that I am surprised we do not discuss more commonly. Clients most often come to us with a problem. They feel like an impostor, they are overwhelmed, their teams are squabbling, they need to make a difficult decision, their health is suffering, and the list goes on. Traditionally, coaches help clients by aiding them in articulating specific goals, exploring resources that might be helpful in making progress toward that goal, and then supporting their progress. In this way, coaches can be every bit as problem-focused as our clients are. Here lies the mismatch: we are often encouraged to "coach the person and not the problem." That is, coaches tend to focus on client process, perception, and learning rather than on the problem looming before the client. Even so, many forces can lead many coaches to coach the problem.

Marcia Reynolds, a thought leader in coaching, describes this in her book that is appropriately called *Coach the Person, Not the Problem*.[1] She makes the argument that coaching works best when we engage clients in reflection. It is through this process that they gain self-knowledge and begin to evolve their thinking in ways that help them craft solutions to their problems. It is a philosophical argument that will, I am certain, resonate with virtually every coach, and I agree with it.

Even so, coaching the person is easier said than done. Because they are so heavily focused on the problems before them, clients often explicitly or unwittingly pull coaches in that direction. They sometimes seek quick solutions, intuitively emphasize planning, and complain about the emotional toll of their challenges. As a result, coaching exists on an event horizon—the boundary of a black hole beyond which nothing can escape—in which we feel the tug to focus on the problem. It is all too easy to find ourselves sucked into the client story, focusing on the singular pressing problem and taking credit for client progress or feeling guilty for client stagnation.

For example, I was training a novice health coach once who felt that her role was to help her client lose weight (her client's agenda). She focused heavily on creating diets, exercise plans, and sleep schedules; marshaling client resources; and holding her client accountable for progress in each of these areas. To some degree, the coaching was effective. The client felt highly supported and, as a result, stayed engaged with the coaching. The client liked the progress she was making and the coach felt good that she was helping. What the coach missed, however, was the fact that she was engaged in a fairly superficial level of coaching support. She was so focused on helping the client solve *this* problem that she overlooked the ways that she might help the client solve *all* similar problems. She did little to explore the client's relationship with her problem, her perception of the problem, the way the client understood her own habits and processes, and the social context in which the problem existed. These types of explorations often yield new insights, fresh identity narratives, and deeper understandings that can be applied well beyond the confines of the problem at hand. We find ourselves attempting to balance support for the client's concerns on the one hand and a wider focus on client insight and learning on the other (see table 4.1).

TABLE 4.1. Costs and benefits of coaching the person versus the problem

	Costs	Benefits
Coaching the problem	Clients miss opportunities for self-knowledge that can lead to wider empowerment and effectiveness.	Clients feel supported and can jump into fast and effective problem-solving.
Coaching the person	Clients can be impatient with this process, frustrated with the "deep" nature of inquiry, and want to ask for advice or focus on nuts-and-bolts planning.	Clients gain the opportunity for general self-knowledge, shifts in perspective, and broader ability to perform beyond a single problem.

It makes sense to wonder whether coaching is indeed about solving problems. That's what clients often want, but—and here might be an example of coaches having a reasonable agenda of their own—there can be far more to coaching than problem-solving. To some extent, this positive provocation is aimed more pointedly at coaches at the beginning of their careers. The tension between engaging clients in self-directed learning and supporting them in solving their problems is one that early stage coaches return to time and again. Even so, this provocation is not exclusive to those coaches. All of us, regardless of years of experience, feel the temptation to pat ourselves on the back when a client succeeds or to double our efforts when a client is stuck. It is common for coaches of any seniority to want to work harder than their clients, and so for more experienced practitioners, I have tried to include some science and discussion that might still be new and provoke new reflection.

A Problem Focus Is Normal

It makes sense that clients focus on their problems rather than on themselves. A problem focus is understandable. In fact, people are hardwired with a pesky problem detector known as the *negativity bias*—our evolutionary birthright that helps us function. People are naturally vigilant for problems, we can easily be made to be cautious, and we are sensitive to setbacks. Problems loom larger in our minds than do the good times. Let's do a little thought experiment to find some evidence for this phenomenon: Think of a time you suffered a physical injury. Next, think of a time when you enjoyed an exceptional moment of happiness. If you are at all like most people, then the negative memory came to mind more quickly, felt highly distinct, and might even have felt more intense. This same negativity bias influences our clients: it informs their agenda, drags their attention, and focuses their plans. As a result, we ought to understand it better.

One of my research heroes is Paul Rozin, a professor of psychology at the University of Pennsylvania. Like a great coach, he has a knack for asking questions that others do not. His studies have focused on the enjoyment of food, the emotion of disgust, fear of moral contamination, and conflict resolution, among others. Relevant to this discussion, he has written about the negativity bias in a way that I think is helpful to coaches.[2] Paul neatly divides negativity biases into distinct types:

Negative potency—This is the idea that negative events are generally more potent than equivalent positive ones. For example, the death of a child generally creates more misery than the birth of a child creates happiness. Similarly, losing our job takes a larger psychological toll than the mental lift we enjoy when getting a job, which is, in part, why coaches spend relatively more time showing empathy and compassion to our clients than we do celebrating with them. Clients focus far more on problems, setbacks, and potential problems than they do on progress, successes, and celebrations.

Negative dominance—This is the idea that when negatives and positives are blended, the negatives are dominant. Imagine you had a delicious and healthy salad, but a cockroach was in it. The presence of that negative cockroach outweighs all the health and taste advantages of the salad. No amount of salad can outweigh that one tiny cockroach. Although this example is absurd, it illustrates this phenomenon nicely, and it actually happened to me at a hotel restaurant. The same holds true in more common scenarios: you can receive three compliments from your team, but you will likely spend more time stewing about the one email you receive that is highly critical of your performance. You need relatively more positives to outweigh the negative in blended scenarios, although no specific ratio likely accomplishes this.

Negative differentiation—This is the idea that people are generally better at differentiating negatives than they are positives. For example, list all the negative emotions you can in one column and then all the positive ones in another. Your negative list is likely to be longer. Next, you will note that the positive ones feel similar. Joy and love, for example, have some experiential overlap. Rage and worry and boredom, by contrast, feel highly distinct from one another.

One more aspect of the negativity bias is related to negativity potency: our general sensitivity to losses, which can be clearly seen in research on prospect theory. Daniel Kahneman, the Nobel Prize–winning psychologist who pioneered behavioral economics, demonstrated that people are more sensitive to potential losses than they are to potential gains.[3] What would it take, for example, for you to enter a game of chance in which you could win or lose money? Let's say I flipped a coin, and if it came up tails, you would lose one hundred dollars. How much would you have to win on heads for you to be willing to play? For most people, the win would have to be larger than the loss.

In 1979, Amos Tversky and Kahneman engaged in a prescient bit of research: they presented alternative versions of a vaccine to see how people might make important real-world health decisions. Scenario A described a disease that would affect 20 percent of the population and a vaccine that would protect 50 percent of those receiving it. Scenario B involved two distinct strains of the disease with equal contagion rates and a vaccine that would completely protect against one strain but offer no prophylaxis against the other. Just so you don't have to do the math, both the vaccines in scenarios A and B reduce an individual's risk from 20 percent to 10 percent (see the percentage of the population infected in figure 4.1, which the research participants did not see). Yet those who heard about scenario B were far more likely to find it attractive (57 percent, as opposed to the 40 percent who heard about scenario A). Why might this be? Scenario B is phrased in a way that creates a sense of uncertainty. In the face of uncertainty, people tend to go negative.

This makes sense from an evolutionary perspective. Interpreting a garden hose as possibly being a snake and jumping back is far less costly than not caring if it is a hose or a snake. As a result, we tend to scan our horizons—socially and physically—for possible threats, problems, obstacles, and setbacks. Clients also walk into sessions focused on threats to their jobs or performance, hung up on setbacks, and worried about failure. Because we want to prioritize their agendas, and because we also have a negativity bias, we are likely to collude in a heavy problem focus.

One last note about the evolutionary nature of our attention and thinking. The negativity bias is not the only bias we have. This

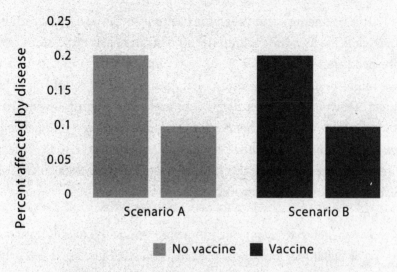

FIGURE 4.1. Infection rates for a hypothetical disease

predilection is, to some degree, counteracted by what is known as the *positivity offset*, which is the idea that our natural resting state is mildly positive and we are ever so slightly inclined to see things positively.[4] In one set of laboratory studies, by way of illustration, people were likely to interpret photos of neutral objects, such as chairs, as if they were positive. Similarly, researchers (including me) have found time and again that most people are mildly happy most of the time. Put simply, in the absence of overt problems, people tend toward the positive, rather than the neutral.

This also makes sense from an evolutionary perspective because happier people are more exploratory, build better social coalitions, are healthier, and are more likely to survive. These turn out to be advantages that allow happier people to reproduce with greater success. In sum, people are not just hand-wringing worriers. We mostly feel upbeat and optimistic and enjoy life. Then, when a problem—or potential problem—comes our way, it looms large and arrests our attention.

This balancing act between the positivity offset and the negativity bias leads me to wonder about the tone of our coaching sessions. Are we needlessly positioning them as problem-solving sessions when we might be using them more often as an exploration of improvement? One potential hazard of this approach is thoughtfully outlined by Mary Beth O'Neill in her book, *Executive Coaching with Backbone and Heart*.[5] In it, she argues that coaches can be lulled into the role of "rescuer" when we align too heavily with clients' problems. O'Neill lists some symptoms of the rescuer mentality:

- A belief that the client cannot solve the problem without you
- A belief that you know more or would do a better job at solving the problem than your client would
- A temptation to offer advice
- A tendency to speak as much as the client or to instruct the client
- A focus on client weaknesses

I would also add taking credit for client success or feeling guilty when clients stagnate or fail. These thoughts and actions are common and troubling enough among coaches that I believe it is worth considering an alternative to the fixer mentality.

The Improvement Mindset

In much of the coaching I have observed, coaches engage clients in problem-based talk, reinforce the idea that obstacles are everywhere, and focus heavily on negatives. Every time coaches ask, "What's holding you back?" or "What would you do if you were not afraid?" they are adopting a problem-focused mindset. Every time they see a self-limiting belief or complain about a should, they are negatively focused. Every time we suggest that clients can use a strength to solve a problem or ask about support they might receive in solving that problem, we are still focusing on problems.

In some ways, I look at the coaching session—with its artificial environment and unique internal rules—as a psychological time-out from problems. In this space, we can say, "Your problems are out there, but we can relax temporarily in here. We can be honest and exploratory and creative." This is where I think drawing a distinction from the problem mindset (which many clients have when they show up for a session) and the improvement mindset (which is more typical of visioning) is important. If we engender the idea that coaching is largely about continuous improvement in the service of desirable goals, then all we care about are steps forward. This emphasis allows for more positivity, visioning, and resource building than does its problem-focused cousin. I even argue that between these two mindset are sweeping differences (see table 4.2).

TABLE 4.2. Fixing versus improving a problem

Fix a problem	Improve on circumstances or skills
Encourages a sense of urgency	Involves a longer timeline
Emphasizes understanding the problem	Emphasizes articulating goals
Places a premium on identifying causes	Places a premium on identifying resources
Encourages identifying and implementing a plan	Encourages experimentation
Results in clients feeling discouraged by failure	Results in clients looking forward to learning
Focuses on negative impacts of the problem if it persists	Focuses on the likely benefits of improvement if it happens

Once I started thinking about the improvement mindset, I began to see ways that I could introduce it into my own coaching sessions. I questioned my own assumptions about my role as a coach. I adopted the solutions-focus adage "Empathize with problems, but try not to invite more problem talk; instead, invite solution talk." I found that I asked more questions, such as "What would you like to improve at?" "What would you like to learn?" and "What would you prefer instead?" Coaches with a solutions-focused orientation will recognize these questions as familiar staples. Indeed, my ideas about improvement versus fixing are heavily ensconced in this approach but are not identical to it.

The other major change in my coaching was that I gave up the idea of homework. Coaches are often eager to identify tasks that clients can perform between sessions to maintain progress toward their goals. All too often, in my opinion, these between-session activities are framed in terms of success and failure. Whether I'm working with clients who want to get to the gym twice in a week or managers who want to have a difficult conversation with their direct report, clients often leave the session thinking, "This will either work or it will not." In creating such a frame for homework, coaches often unwittingly set up our clients for potential psychological distress in case their plans don't work out. Didn't get to the gym? It feels like a failure. That tough conversation went off the rails? A failure, at least in the mind of the client.

I still believe in client reflection and action between sessions but I now reframe homework and accountability as experiments. In fact, I do so overtly. I don't ask, "What would you like to do between now and next session?" or "How would you like to apply the learning from this session?" Instead, I opt for "What would you like to experiment with?" This phrase clearly emphasizes the learning process that is at the heart of all coaching. My clients understand that they are tinkering, not performing, and that they can take away valuable lessons, regardless of what happens. They understand that they are on a road to iterative improvements rather than fixing their problems.

Is There a Real Difference?

We can easily dismiss a problem-versus-improvement focus as a mere linguistic shell game. Critics might argue that whatever we call it, we are essentially employing the same coaching techniques, and clients are essentially deriving the same benefit. This is where empirical inquiry comes in: by testing each approach scientifically, we can begin to see patterns of evidence suggesting that these approaches are indeed more than a case of "a rose by any other name would smell as sweet." In fact, time and again, we see the needle moving toward the benefits of a solutions-focused orientation.

The late coach Anthony Grant was a key figure in establishing the field of coaching psychology. He was the first person in history to receive a doctorate in that topic, and he helped found the University of Sydney's well-regarded coach training unit. Tony also conducted a number of studies in which he compared problem-focused and solutions-focused coaching. You can see an overview of the studies and their results in table 4.3. They all point to the same conclusion: focusing on desirable improvements appears widely beneficial, if not superior to a narrower focus on solving problems. Admittedly, these studies employ samples of university students and a coach-like (rather than actual coaching) design. Even so, I think the results of this research are sufficiently strong that it makes sense to be open to an improvement or solution approach in your own coaching.

Conclusion

It is tempting to think that, as coaches, we are engaged in a highly positive cause. I believe coaching is a noble pursuit, and I laud those

TABLE 4.3. Research on solutions-focused coaching

Year	Participants and methods	Results
2010[6]	74 students responding in writing to problem- or solutions-focused questions	Both approaches were helpful; a solutions-focus increased self-efficacy, insight, and positive emotions.
2012[7]	225 students, same as above	Results of the 2010 study were replicated.
2018[8]	512 students, as above but added a "positive affect" condition in which participants were induced into a good mood	Results of earlier studies were replicated and extended by finding that simply being in a good mood is not enough to enhance self-efficacy. When good moods were paired with solutions-focused approaches, the best outcomes occurred (self-efficacy and number of action steps taken toward problem).
2019[9]	80 students, same as above but with a combined problem- and solution-focused condition	A solutions-focused approach alone produced greater goal attainment and self-efficacy than a problem-focused or combined approach.

with a helping mentality. Even so, I am surprised at how negative much of coaching is. We often unwittingly collude with our clients to carve away all the problems rather than building all that is good. We organize sessions around client problems, we focus on weaknesses, we explore setbacks, we predict challenges, and we fight against self-limiting beliefs. I've never seen a study that counts the frequency of coaches saying words like *problem, difficulty, obstacle,* and *stuck,* but I suspect that none of us would like the results. The risk of this natural tendency is that we can fall into a rescuing mentality, myopically focus on a granular problem, or rob the client of opportunities for more generalizable empowerment.

In this context, we should consider an alternative: coaching is about improvement, not problem-solving. Clients want to grow, master, evolve, and change for the better. When we focus our discussion there, the sessions are potentially more engaging for the client and might leave them with a greater sense of self-efficacy. We can draw on some simple principles from solution-focus coaching, such as accepting problem-based talk (even showing compassion toward it) but not inviting more of it, engaging clients in defining what desirable life they would prefer rather than what awful conditions they would like to avoid, and focusing on experimentation and learning over problem-solving plans and homework.

REFLECT AND EXPERIMENT

- Try ditching homework as a between-session action. Instead, frame it as conducting an experiment that might be successful to greater or lesser degrees. Emphasize the importance of learning from the trial.
- If you record your sessions, watch a ten-minute portion and count the number of times you use negative or problem-focused language versus the number of times you mention solutions, improvement, enthusiasm, or other positive language.
- Reflect on your own coaching philosophy regarding the importance of addressing problems versus engaging clients in a process of personal learning and improvement. Imagine you were training novice coaches. How would you describe the work of a coach to this group with the problem-versus-improvement tension in mind?

Why Are Ethics So Boring?

LIKE MANY coaches, I enjoy receiving ongoing training to develop my skills and insights into my professional practice. To this end, I register for a number of courses, workshops, and conferences each year. Just a few years ago, I had the opportunity to participate with a group of fifteen experienced coaches as we coached one another and discussed basic skills. We examined the nuance of metaphor and silence and then, a few weeks into our time together, we addressed the topic of ethics. The group's facilitator opened by asking, "What one word comes up for you when you think of ethics?" I have asked this same question to hundreds—perhaps even thousands—of coaches over the years. Although the answers vary, they tend to be along a theme: *important, responsibility, integrity, rigid,* and *rules* are some of the most common responses I have heard. In this particular group of fifteen, however, eleven people said *boring.* I glanced down at the word I had written: *fascinating.*

It's true. I find ethics exciting. When I was pursuing graduate studies in clinical psychology, I became fascinated by ethics in psychotherapy. My peers and I learned the guiding principles, such as *nonmalfeasance* (avoid harm) and *beneficence* (promote welfare). What I remember most, however, is our endless discussions over questions that had no definitive answers. Should a therapist accept a gift from a client? Should a therapist conduct a session if they are feeling ill, or is it worse to cancel? In every case, the answer was "It depends." "It depends," in my opinion, is one of the least satisfying answers in the history of answers. I hear it all the time from coaches, and all I can think is "You're only halfway there; now complete the thought. What exactly does it depend upon?" In graduate school, our meandering discussions of the myriad factors on which such decisions depend made me a more responsible professional. By thinking through the "It depends" response, I became able to articulate why accepting a gift could be perfectly fine in one instance and what the potential hazards were in other instances.

I was so enchanted by the topic, in fact, that I wrote my master's thesis, "Legal and Ethical Dilemmas Related to Confidentiality in Psychotherapy." I know! Not exactly a beach read. This brings us right back to the fact that I wrote *fascinating* while three-quarters of the group wrote *boring*. I'll be the first to admit, ethics does not have a reputation for being exciting, and that is exactly what I want to change in this provocation.

What Are Ethics, Anyway?

The word *ethics* comes from the Greek word *ethos*, meaning "character." When Aristotle wrote the *Nicomachean Ethics*, he was writing a treatise about how a person should live.[1] This emphasis on right action is more than some know-it-all wagging a finger at "kids these days." It includes the idea that when we make virtuous and intentional choices, we are able to—according to Aristotle—be more civically engaged, better able to live up to our own potential, and able to fully experience the good life. This notion of right action is also not merely the product of Western civilization. African philosophies, Confucian teaching, and Hinduism—to give just three examples—are all equally focused on making good decisions and behaving well according to local standards.

This universal hunt for good character gave rise to modern professional ethics. In professional circles, associations adopt ethical principles as well as ethical standards. The former are broad principles, such as client autonomy, that provide a values framework for making decisions. Ethical principles are included in every professional code of conduct ranging from those of medical doctors to coaches. They are not enforceable. The rules-oriented portion of ethical codes are the ethical standards. These include specific behaviors, such as maintaining confidentiality, that professionals are required to engage in.

When people think of ethical codes, they often focus on the standards rather than the principles. Perhaps this causes people to have such an at-arm's-length relationship with ethics. Their view of the topic is similar to their view of the printed rules for board games: boring and strict but there if we ever need to look something up. By contrast, I believe that both principles and standards have the same aim: to help guide our decisions when making such choices is difficult. That is, ethics is all about a decision-making process. Here are three elements of ethical thinking that I think make the topic slightly more interesting.

Ethics Are Aspirational, Not Prohibitive

People often view ethical codes as long lists of prohibitions. Don't divulge a client's name. Don't go into business with a client. Don't make promises you cannot deliver on. Don't portray yourself as more qualified than you actually are. Don't. Don't. Don't. Ethics become less constricting as soon as we flip that notion and realize that they are about aspirational behaviors. Do hold your client's confidentiality tightly. Do keep your professional roles clearly defined. Do make promises on which you can deliver. Do portray your qualifications accurately. Do. Do. Do. In fact, the aspirational nature of ethics is so important that the ICF revised one of its standards in 2020: "I adhere to the philosophy of 'doing good' versus 'avoiding bad.'"[2]

Ethics Are about Personal Judgment, Not Totalitarian Control

The widespread perception of ethics as being heavy, burdensome, or rigid stems from the idea that they are external fences that pen in professionals. Look again, and you will see that in every instance, you have a fair amount of room for personal judgment calls. For example, coaches are mandated to continue personal and professional development, but how we can go about doing this includes a wide degree of latitude. Similarly, we are mandated to accurately identify our coaching qualifications and experience. Sounds easy, right? I once knew a coach who had done work in two nations—let's say it was Canada and South Africa. On her website, however, she wrote, "From work in Canada to work in South Africa, I have a wide range of coaching experience." This statement likely fulfills the letter of the law, but it also knowingly misleads because it strongly suggests that she has a host of unmentioned experience. To me, these situations are where ethics becomes the most exciting—in our autonomy to deeply think through such issues and to make judgment calls.

Ethics Concern Ambiguity, Not Certainty

I like to think of ethical codes as embodying guiding principles to help us think through ambiguous situations. If I ask ten coaches if they think they should have a sexual relationship with their clients, I will likely hear ten strong negative responses. If, on the other hand, I ask ten coaches if they think it is permissible to have a friendly lunch with a client, I am more likely to hear five voices in favor and five against. Although coaches do occasionally break the black-and-white taboos, such as having sex with clients, professionals mostly get into trouble in the gray areas. Virtually every aspect of our profession is shrouded in uncertainty, and having principles and standards can help guide our thinking.

Let me give you an example from my own practice. I often use examples such as case studies when I train coaches, and I have witnessed two things: First, people often have strong and certain reactions about what to do in each circumstance. The answer can seem so clear as to be obvious. Second, the solution that seems so clearly right is never unanimous. Members of groups always disagree with one another. If anything, this illustrates why we need a tool for thinking through the issues.

Here's the scenario: Early in my coaching career, I was approached by a prospective client who wanted to write a tell-all book about her sexual abuse (her words). She was a survivor of childhood abuse and felt that her mission was to speak out about it, largely in the hopes of inspiring others who might suffer similar abuse. She reassured me that she had decades of therapy under her belt and was not seeking a therapeutic outlet for her trauma. She knew I had written several books, and so she thought I might be able to support her through the book-writing process. Here's the question: Should I take her on as a client? Roughly half of my trainees say that it is perfectly fine to do so, and roughly half worry that there are too many psychological booby traps.

By turning to principles and standards, we can think through the major thematic issues in this case. First, let's consider the principle of avoiding harm. Regardless of whether the prospective client had previously attended therapy, she still risks psychological distress that can come up when writing such a book. In addition, we had to weigh foreseeable legal and social dangers related to such a book. She reported that she had not consulted a lawyer. I also worried about scope-of-practice issues. In part, the woman wanted a consultant to explain to her how book proposals are put together. In part, the work itself was a therapeutic project, even if it was not psychotherapy. Taken together, these concerns caused me to decline to work with her—not because her story was false or that she wasn't worthwhile or she didn't have a laudable goal but because I treat yellow lights like red lights. With enough cautionary indications, I don't go forward.

Why Don't We Focus More on Ethics?

Professional ethics is a basic requirement of all coach training, whether by becoming credentialed through the Association for Coaching, the National Board for Health and Wellness Coaches, the European Mentoring and Coaching Council, or another organization. Not only is ethics integrated into basic coach training, it is typically mandated as part of continuing professional education. Why don't we hear more about it then?

I believe coaches experience three major obstacles when trying to engage more actively with the topic of ethics. Sure, some may encounter two or four or more obstacles, but I've identified three major ones here.

"I Go with My Gut"

I have rarely come across a profession that more overtly lionizes intuition as does coaching. Doctors and therapists talk about clinical intuition, but most professions seem to focus heavily on identifiable technique rather than instinct. Coaching is distinct in this regard. I hear coaches say, "It just felt right," "It emerged in the moment," or other statements that prioritize intuition and hard-to-pin-down insights. I'm not dismissing intuition, but I believe it is problematic in the context of professional ethics. Some coaches might not feel obliged to wed themselves to a formal ethical code because they feel they have an internal compass that accurately measures good and bad.

Here's the problem with the go-with-your-gut mentality: your gut is effective only as a rule-out mechanism and not as a rule-in one. Consider this: if you feel some misgivings about an element of working with a client, these niggling doubts are highly worth listening to. Typically, the moral doubt you experience should give you pause. On the other hand, a lot of things that feel right are still not right. In the end, I argue that going with your gut is great to rule out something doubtful but is far less effective as a tool for green-lighting work.

"I'm Not Planning on Doing Anything Wrong"

A few years before his passing, my father had to renew his driver's license. One of the questions on the test that he got wrong dealt with the possible penalties for driving drunk. He complained to me, "How should I know what the penalties are? Is it important that I know? I don't drink and drive!" This sentiment is understandable and is linked to what some coaches think. "What do I need a code of ethics for," they muse, "if I am not planning to break confidentiality or have sex with my clients?" This line of reasoning errs toward making issues black and white and underestimates the many gray-area problems that arise.

As another example, many coaches offer standard packages of services without any real consultation with their new clients. These coaches say, "I offer four sessions for X amount" rather than asking, "What number of sessions makes sense for us?" The latter approach is directly linked to the co-created ethos of coaching. In the broadest possible sense, this could be considered an ethical issue because coaches unwittingly overstep by offering standard packages: they believe they know better than their clients, they prioritize their own financial security over what might be best for clients, and they engage in uncritical practice. Assuming that you will face tough choices, rather than framing potential situations as if you might "do things wrong," opens the door to the idea that we all need to engage in ethical thinking.

"I Don't Agree with Current Ethical Standards"

In many instances, coaches are critical of professional coaching organizations and their codes of ethics. I know this to be true because I am one of those coaches. For example, the ICF ethics code includes the following: "Disclose to my clients the potential receipt of compensation and other benefits I may receive for referring my clients to third parties."[3] Personally, I think kickbacks for third-party referrals cannot be trusted. As soon as I receive compensation for making a referral, I can no longer be completely certain that my referral is objectively my best recommendation for the client. Personally, I would not accept third-party compensation for a referral, even though this transaction is allowable under the formal code of ethics. Having said that, I do not believe that minor points of departure are a strong rationale for avoiding an ethical code. In fact, thinking through the extent to which you agree with each ethical standard is extraordinarily helpful in developing ethical thinking.

Implications for Coaches

Each year, the American Alpine Club publishes a book called *Accidents in North American Climbing*. In three-to-four-page vignettes, it describes the various accidents that have occurred that resulted in death or serious injury. This book is not meant to satisfy some morbid curiosity but instead offers a helpful breakdown of what went wrong, such as inexperience, improper equipment, poor decisions, or bad luck. Climbers can benefit from this annual publication because it acts as a reminder that the readers are just like those who end up in trouble. The book also provides a step-by-step breakdown of the problems. I have always wished that coaching had an analogous publication called *Accidents in Coaching Ethics*.

The closest we come is the ICF's annual *Ethical Conduct and Compliance Report*. This three-to-four-page report reviews the number of complaints filed (thirty-two in the 2020 report), as well as the number that met the requirements for initial review (seventeen of thirty-two) and the number that the review board ultimately dealt with (eight). Of those, only a single coach was found in breach of ethical compliance. The complaint, in this case, was that the coach acted in an unprofessional, harmful, and racially biased way. Apart from that, we have no information whatsoever about what happened. As a coach trainer, this lack of information limits my ability to effectively use real-world case studies to help my students recognize ethical blind spots and improve their thinking about ethical issues.

My first recommendation for coaches, then, is that we pick up the slack by collating our own case studies for distribution and discussion. I have been doing this for years. My case studies are not dramatic events. They do not involve embezzling money or sexual relationships. Instead, they consist of small issues: a client invites you to a barbecue, you terminate with a client but then have the opportunity to coach their spouse, you have the opportunity to work with a company from an industry that you have a strong values stance against, a colleague reveals some identifying information about their client, and the list goes on.

These types of cases arise periodically, and coaches who are involved in peer supervision groups (which meet regularly to discuss practice) can benefit from discussing these case studies. I would estimate that I have a conversation about a real ethical issue approximately once every six weeks. I double-checked this figure with my sister, who is a clinical supervisor of therapists. She agreed that, for her profession, the number is similar: she recommends that private practice therapists engage in peer consultation around ethical issues about every four to six weeks. This sentiment is a fairly widely held opinion: thought leaders in coaching endorse the idea of receiving supervision and engaging in peer support networks.[4]

My other recommendation is that you develop a clear framework for making ethical decisions. Many such models exist. Some have six steps while others have twelve. They all emphasize being aware of ethical issues and understanding who is involved and the potential harms, and they all encourage us to seek out advice and weigh options. My colleague Christian van Nieuwerburgh and I have come up with an easy-to-remember framework that we call *the four Cs*. Whenever you find yourself scratching your head about a particular coaching decision, consult your contract, code of ethics, colleagues, and your own personal core values. Taken together, these four sources of information can help you think through decisions in the most responsible way possible.

REFLECT AND EXPERIMENT

- What are your own intuitions about the prevalence of ethical lapses in coaching? How often do you believe they occur?
- In what specific ways has your coaching improved over the last two years? What might you say to a coach who could not effectively answer this question?
- Who do you go to to discuss tough issues in coaching? How often does this occur?
- When was the last time you conducted an ethical audit of your coaching practice? Where might you have blind spots in your marketing, pricing, self-knowledge, cultural sensitivity, or client interactions?

Should Coaches Study Learning Theory?

OVER COACHING'S relatively short history, a number of pioneers and thought leaders have also offered succinct definitions of what we do. For example, Elaine Cox, Tatiana Bachkirova, and David Clutterbuck suggest coaching is "a human development process that involves structured, focused interactions and the use of appropriate strategies, tools, and techniques to promote desirable and sustainable change for the benefit of the coachee and potentially for other stakeholders."[1] Sir John Whitmore proposes that coaching is "unlocking people's potential to maximize performance. Helping them to learn rather than teaching them."[2]

I love the emphasis on learning in that last one. At the risk of disagreeing with founding father Whitmore, I would argue that coaches are, in fact, teachers. By *teacher*, I do not mean the stereotype of a college professor standing at a podium and lecturing. Teaching is no more telling than learning is listening. If that were the case, you would remember every TED Talk you had ever watched. When I listen to people describe TED Talks, however, it often sounds like this: "I saw this great TED Talk! The speaker was a neuroscientist from Harvard or Yale or somewhere. She was amazing. She said that, like, your brain can change." That's not much actual learning. I don't mean to come down too hard on TED Talks; I am just using them as a foil to underscore the point.

When I suggest that coaches are teachers, I mean it in the sense that every experienced educator will understand: teachers are facilitators of the acquisition of knowledge and skill. Coaches also facilitate learning. One major difference is that teachers tend to have studied learning theory, instructional design, and other pedagogical and andragogical tools, and coaches mostly have not. This provocation is my call to arms to think more about learning in coaching.

What Are Your Intuitions about Learning?

Take a moment to consider a time when you learned something. Maybe you were training to be a coach or taking up the cello, Italian cooking, or sign language. Perhaps you were learning about the history of Uganda, the rules of rugby, or Jean Piaget's stages of cognitive development. Consider the mechanisms by which you were able to learn whatever subject you chose to focus on. What insights does this give you about the learning process?

Most people operate under some assumptions—often unconscious—about how learning works, including these examples:

- Perhaps you think that people are repositories that can be filled when information is transferred from one person to another. This is similar to the *blank slate* idea offered by John Locke.
- Perhaps you believe that learning happens when cues and reinforcement play a role in behavior change. This idea is called, appropriately enough, *behaviorism*.
- Maybe you think that people use their existing mental models to help find a sensible mental space for new information. This theory is known as *constructivist learning*.

My point is that the process of learning can add a level of sophistication to your coaching. Some coaches are stuck at the level of believing that asking questions is what evokes new insights. Although I largely agree with the idea that questions and insights can be linked, this way of thinking sheds little light on the learning process.

By contrast, consider the following idea. You likely use some combination of the various learning theories mentioned above. When you check in with clients at the beginning of a session and celebrate their progress, you are reinforcing them through behaviorism. When you ask questions such as "What might make this task more enjoyable?" you are using emotion as a proxy for positive reinforcement—again, a form of behaviorism. When you inquire about past instances in which your clients might have successfully navigated a similar problem, you are leaning constructivist. When you feel the urge to explain something to clients, the blank slate theory is at play. Realizing all of this can place a renewed emphasis on the ways that you, as a coach, are facilitating and reinforcing client learning.

Adult Learning and Coaching

Most educational scholars agree that adult learning differs from child learning in that it works best when it has the following attributes:

Self-directed—This form of learning occurs in a direction, style, and pace laid out by the learner. Coaching is a hand-in-glove fit with this because of its emphasis on the client directing the agenda.

Emphasis on experiential learning—Because adults already have large webs of knowledge, they can employ trial and error and feedback to learn through doing. This reinforces the notion that the so-called homework that takes place between sessions is especially useful when portrayed as experimentation and an opportunity to learn rather than as achieving a goal.

Linked to real-world application—Again, coaching typically addresses links between insight and application with questions such as "How might you use this new learning?" and "What would you like to do with this insight?"

Although most coaches intuitively or explicitly attend to these elements of adult learning, these other areas might go unaddressed:

Anticipation—In instructional theory, the concept known as *anticipatory set* is, in essence, the way that an educator can prep a learning mindset by signaling the anticipated lesson. When I train coaches, I do this through a tool known as a *learning anticipation guide* (LAG). The LAG for each lesson offers some statements that might be true, partially true, or false. My students make guesses about the veracity of each statement and then provide their rationale for each guess. Doing so signals to them the topic that is about to be covered as well as some of the main questions and themes related to this topic. What's more, they can return to their LAG after completing each lesson to evaluate the extent to which their initial instincts were correct. In this way, they have a clear idea about how their thinking has changed as a result of the lesson (in other words, what they learned). You can create an anticipatory set in your coaching sessions as well (and perhaps you already do). When you are setting the session agenda and you ask questions such as "What themes do you anticipate will come up for you during this discussion?" or "What are you most curious about regarding this issue?" you are engaging the client's learning mindset.

Emotion—Although everyone experiences emotions, many people are relatively unfamiliar with a secondary class of feelings that psychologists refer to as *knowledge emotions*. As the name suggests, these feelings stimulate exploration, reflection, and overall learning. The knowledge emotions include boredom, interest, surprise, and confusion. Surprise focuses attention when something in the environment is unexpected. Interest helps people engage with novel, odd, or unfamiliar things. People feel interested when they are dealing with something highly novel that they also feel they can potentially comprehend. Confusion occurs under the same circumstances, but the person feels the topic is difficult to comprehend.

Imagine I show two people the abstract artwork of Jackson Pollock. Kendra might find the paint splashes gimmicky and confusing. She might say, "A child could do that!" because she has little frame of reference for understanding art in general and no clear criteria for evaluating artistic merit beyond personal preference. Kendra is likely to disengage with Pollock's art, perhaps dismissing it as difficult to understand or lacking in quality. By contrast, Latif might think the art is wonderful because he already has an existing web of knowledge about Dadaism, surrealism, and cubism. This preexisting knowledge helps Latif frame Pollock's work in a chronology of abstract painting and better appreciate the contributions Pollock's work had and continues to have on modern art.

The same holds true with your clients. At times, they will be highly emotionally invested in the coaching discussion because they feel hopeful that their problems can be solved, excited by new insights, and interested in where the conversation might head. At other times, however, they might disengage because they feel the problems are simply difficult to understand or solve. Recognizing the role of emotions in the coaching session can help you to explore them, understand your client's experience, and better engage their learning. When clients express forms of confusion, for instance, it can be helpful to focus on growing their capacity to cope with problems rather than on the problem itself.

SHOULD COACHES STUDY LEARNING THEORY? 51

Conclusion

This provocation is not intended to supply an overview of all educational theory or instructional design. Instead, I hope to have sparked your interest in the topic by framing coaching fundamentally as a learning endeavor rather than a goal pursuit. Once you consider learning (and its application) to be the core tenet of coaching, it opens the idea that knowing more about learning can improve your coaching. Imagine how your coaching might leapfrog forward if you knew more about interleaving, elaboration, spaced practice, or other strategies for effective learning. This is why I increasingly believe that coaches should have learning theory incorporated into their training or—if not—into their continuing education.

REFLECT AND EXPERIMENT

- After each session, track your clients' insights. This might be instances in which your clients said, "Good question" or in the list of takeaways they recounted at the end of the session. For each of these moments of learning, consider the various factors that might have influenced them. Consider also how you might link to and reinforce these in subsequent sessions.
- Play around with the idea of an anticipatory set in the beginning of your session. What might you be able to do in the early stages of the session that will foster a learning mindset, increase curiosity, and signal the potential for learning?
- Pay attention to emotion as a context in which learning occurs. This might include your coaching sessions, your children's learning (if you have any), or your own learning. Which emotions seem to be part of the process? How often do you notice confusion? How closely linked is emotion to the moment of learning? How is it linked?

PART TWO
Communicating with Clients

C OACHING is, at its heart, a conversational technology. Since coaching is a discussion between (usually) two people, the ability to communicate effectively is vital to effective coaching. It is not too great a leap to suggest that people who have a decent amount of social intelligence and verbal acumen are better positioned to be coaches than those who do not. In fact, the best coaches are, in my opinion, master communicators. They lean into language in playful ways such as using metaphor. They tend to be better-than-average listeners. They are surprisingly comfortable with silence.

In my experience, people who sign up for coach training do so because they are interested in gaining the coaching skills to help others. What they often do not realize—and what many of them trumpet as the best part of training—is how profoundly coach training affects communication. Trainees reflect on different types of questions, pay greater attention to word choice, and tolerate silence, often for the very first time.

It is no wonder, then, that coaches have adopted a number of attitudes toward communication. Collectively, we give a thumbs-up to some practices while we tend to frown on others. This part deals with exactly these leanings. It starts by tackling the common prohibition against asking so-called why questions. From there, the provocations move on to interruption (maybe we should do more of it?) and using the client's language (maybe we should do less of it?). In the fourth provocation in this section, I introduce the concept of symmetries and asymmetries in coaching questions. The last two provocations are a musing about the role of small talk in coaching sessions and a reflection on the optimal amount of silence we might use.

As a minor note of backstory, one of the provocations in this part provoked me even as I wrote it. I created my initial draft and then had an argument with myself, completely changed my mind, and wrote the revised provocation arguing the exact opposite of what I had first intended. See if you can guess which one it is.

PROVOCATION 7

Why Ask Why?

IF YOU have spent even a month in the world of coaching or in coach training, you have undoubtedly come across the prohibition against asking why questions. Recently, Ian Day traced the history of this admonition and found *no* source for it.[1] There is no record of any thought leader or pioneer in coaching advocating a strong "Don't ask why" position. And yet this urban myth endures.

One explanation is that some coaches feel these questions are judgmental, as if asking "Why would you do that?" is akin to "Why on Earth would you choose to do such a silly thing?" I have never found this rationale particularly compelling for several reasons. First, I am not certain if it is even true. If I am coaching a client who is considering two job offers, and I ask why they are leaning toward one of them, I am not overly worried that they will find my question judgmental or dismissive. This is because of the second issue I have: it's all in tone of voice. If I wrinkle my nose in disgust and screech, "Why?" then, sure, my client will be taken aback. But if I lift my eyebrows, smile, and ask, "Why?" my client is likely to react positively to my curiosity.

The second explanation I have heard for the prohibition against asking why is that alternatives to reaching the same objective are available. Using the earlier example of my client deciding between equally attractive job offers in New York and London, I can ask, "Why is London currently more attractive to you?" in several other ways:

- "What is so attractive about the London job?"
- "What is your rationale for your leaning?"
- "What about the London job speaks to you?"
- "What are the factors influencing this leaning?"

In each case, I feel this is much ado about nothing. The four example alternative questions all ask basically the same thing, and they will most likely yield roughly the same information that "Why London?" will. It is perfectly fine to experiment with alternatives, but I am not convinced that they are inherently superior because they do not start with *why*.

The third caution—and the one I find to be the most compelling—is the possibility that asking why often pushes clients to fabricate a convenient and simple causal explanation. The idea is that the client's story isn't wrong but rather that they are giving a *story*—that is, a particular framing of a causal explanation. If, for instance, I ask you why you have such a passion for lifelong learning, we will get useful and interesting information out of that. But it won't be "the truth" in the same sense that gravity is true. Instead, your answer will be a story you tell yourself about your growth and development and identity. These stories can yield good fodder for conversation, but as a coach, I don't have to buy into their completeness. Instead, I realize that this problem, at its heart, deals with "levels of analysis," problem, which suggests that simultaneous truths are present, but each exists on a different level and requires unique tools to examine.

Let's use an example of real human behavior to illustrate this concept. Imagine Houda, a health coaching client from Toronto. Houda loves the dessert tiramisu even though she knows it is loaded with sugar (which she is working hard to avoid). She eats frequently and then feels guilty about doing so. If, as her coach, I were to ask Houda why she does this, she could certainly offer some explanatory story. She might tell me that she grew up in a house where she was allowed to eat many sweets. What she almost certainly would not say is that her sweet tooth is a complex interaction of cultural, social, personal, genetic, and other causes. However, if we step back and realize that several influences exist at many levels of analysis, we would see that this is indeed the case, as shown in table 7.1.

Many coaches I meet are tempted to treat the genetic, biological, and neuroscientific aspects of behavior as "truer" than perceptive, emotional, or behavioral ones. Remember, these distinct levels of

TABLE 7.1. Levels of analysis

Levels of analysis	Example
Societal/cultural	Dessert is widely available and is a standard part of many meals.
Social/interpersonal	Houda's friends all eat dessert and encourage her to do the same.
Phenomenological/experiential	Houda is aware that dessert reliably gives her short bursts of energy, salves her worries, and is delicious.
Behavioral	Houda has the habit of eating dessert in the evenings when she returns home from work; she purchases dessert on her way home.
Personality	Houda is a somewhat impulsive person who makes quick decisions and loves to take action rather than engage in careful planning.
Genetic/biological	Sugar releases dopamine, elevates blood glucose levels, and stimulates the pancreas to release insulin.

analysis occur simultaneously, and deeper levels of analysis are not truer than others. For example, I don't need to know about oxytocin to be convinced that I love my children. When Houda offers a story about her family of origin, it provides useful but incomplete information. In the end, asking Houda why elicits good information about her mindset, identity, and experience. So long as the coach remembers that her explanation is not the whole story, it can be a useful question.

I am left with the nagging feeling that we are asking the wrong question of ourselves. Instead of asking, "Why shouldn't we ask why?" I would prefer to ask, "Why might we ask why?" I have been thinking of answers to this question and love to hear from others who might round out my thinking further. Table 7.2 and the list below describe a few instances I have noted in which why questions might work well:

- *When challenging the explanatory story might be helpful*— Occasionally, our clients' explanatory stories leave them feeling bad, imprisoned, or wronged. Bringing such stories to light can be the first step in swapping them for healthier stories if

TABLE 7.2. Reasons for and against asking why

Reasons not to ask why	Reasons to ask why
It can sound critical or dismissive.	It can sound curious.
There may be a superior way to get the same information.	It offers a direct way to ask about a client's rationale, evidence, and perception.
It pushes the client to offer an explanatory story.	Hearing a client's explanatory story can be useful.
It reinforces the notion of a single cause that, if identified, can unlock a problem.	It can be used effectively to identify multiple influences and thereby highlight many options for action.

doing so is relevant to the coaching agenda. Asking a question such as "Why do you think you have this pattern of behavior?" is less a fact-finding mission and more of a dowsing rod for the client's personal experience and explanation.

- *When promoting client awareness*—Client stories such as "My supervisor is a jerk" sometimes have limited utility. By addressing levels of analysis, clients often become aware of more nuance and have more points of entry for intervention. Asking a question such as "Why do you think your supervisor acts the way they do?" can lead to a story that your client has constructed ("He was born that way" or "He loves to see other people suffer"). This question can also be the gateway to follow-ups such as "What other factors do you think influence the way your supervisor shows up at work?" Often, these types of questions yield alternative explanations ("He is cranky because he has a newborn and isn't sleeping much" or "He never had good management modeled for him").

- *When clarifying client preferences or decisions*—Simply asking, "Why that one?" in a curious way is often the quickest way to get clients to articulate their current thinking. Whether they are choosing between jobs, new hires, or strategies for giving critical feedback, you can ask, "Why that one?" to get to the heart of their thoughts and feelings. It simply asks for clients' current rationale, leanings, and thinking.

REFLECT AND EXPERIMENT

- Try asking why and play close attention to both the client's response to the question and also the types of information that the question yields.

- Make a list for yourself of the various reasons you might legitimately ask your client a why question.
- Pay attention to conversations in your own life. Note when friends, family members, and colleagues ask why. Note their tone and rationale. Note the way that people react to such questions.

What's So Great about Interrupting?

I AM an active conversationalist, which is a diplomatic way of saying that I tend to interject and interrupt. I was raised in a family (all academics) in which the conversation was the primary unit of inter-action. Everyone in my family confidently expresses strong opinions and feels comfortable debating them, discussing them, and even modifying them in the face of a superior argument. This serves me well in certain contexts, but it can also put off others.

When I first started coaching, I noticed that many of my peers were cut from a different cloth. They were natural listeners. They seemed to be able to effortlessly stay silent and give huge amounts of space for client reflections and reactions—an admirable quality and one I have put a great deal of time into emulating. By contrast, I have seen many of these great listeners struggle with the skill that comes so naturally to me: interrupting.

Understanding Interruption

Some coaches have a strong and negative reaction against the idea of interruption, so I would like to veer from coaching for a moment to discuss research in linguistics. Linguists have studied an aspect of communication known as *overlapping speech*. Normally, conversations are organized around turns, with the speaker taking their turn to speak and the listener remaining silent. Occasionally, however, the listener speaks at the same time as the speaker. Not all of these have the rude quality of an interruption. In fact, you do many of them, even in your coaching. Although many coaches do not realize it, when they say "Mm-hmm" while their client is speaking, this is overlapping speech, an interruption of sorts. Table 8.1 shows several types, three of which are reported by linguist Emanuel Schegloff.[1]

It turns out several psychological mechanisms influence whether a person (or people from a particular culture) are comfortable with overlapping speech, including the following:

- *Relationship to silence*—Cultures that are more comfortable with silence have a higher tolerance for long pauses.

TABLE 8.1. Types of interruption

Type of overlapping speech	Definition
Terminal overlap	Stealing the turn away from the speaker to offer your own thoughts
Continuers	Saying "mm-hmm," "I see," or other phrases meant to communicate understanding
Conditional access to a turn	Briefly offering a forgotten name or word to the speaker or asking a clarifying question before it is your turn to speak
Parallel talk	Interjecting with jokes and starting side conversations or other verbalizations that might redirect the conversation

- *Perceptions of pausing*—Speakers from high-overlap cultures perceive even a tiny pause as the speaker ending their turn and, as a result, are more likely to jump in.
- *Intention of interruption*—They can be either intrusive or collaborative in nature.

To put these into a real-world context, consider a study in which Deborah Tannen investigated the conversational style of Jewish people from New York.[2] The people in her study were likely to introduce new topics and tangents and would sometimes interject to do so. What's more, they felt empowered to make repeated bids to redirect the conversation. Tannen specifically says that, in her experience, New Yorkers are more likely to talk along with the speaker to show how enthusiastically they are listening. What's more, they are highly sensitive to tiny pauses and use these as opportunities to speak up. The very aspects of conversation that outsiders might consider rude are, among New Yorkers, seen as signs of engagement and good listening.

This dynamic is the verbal opposite of an Inuit birthday party I once attended in northern Greenland. Over the course of two hours, almost no one spoke. No one felt any pressure to chat, and merely spending time together was gift enough. This dovetails with Tannen's own experience with native Alaskans living above the Arctic Circle. She writes that some people "get to know people by talking to them, while Athabaskans tend to prefer silence until they feel they know each other."[3] Taken together, the point isn't that native people are good communicators and that New Yorkers are awful but rather that each culture has its own norms for what constitutes an interruption and when these interjections are disruptive versus helpful.

Interruption in Coaching

Bringing this all back to coaching, we can identify several important lessons. I once heard the well-known coach David Peterson explain that he had experimented with interrupting by seeing how frequently he could do it before it became off-putting to clients. He found that one or two interruptions didn't step on a client's toes. More than that, however, and clients became frustrated. This might serve as a permission slip to experiment with interruption. Another justification can be found in the fact that coaches interrupt all the time. When you say "Mm-hmm" to indicate your agreement, you are overlapping. When you interject with a little "That's great!" or "Congratulations," you are similarly interrupting. This insight, for me, changes the question from "Should coaches interrupt?" to "How should coaches interrupt?"

In what circumstances might we strategically choose to interrupt?

Avoiding rambling and repetition—Occasionally, I see coaches give so much space for reflection that clients are not certain what to do. The client has answered the question, and still, the coach remains silent. In the absence of the coach jumping in, the client continues to talk just to fill the uncomfortable space, often repeating or rewording what they have already said.

Backstory—Clients often assume that we need backstory to coach effectively. People are naturally storytelling creatures, and we tend to lay out ideas in narrative form: "First this happened, and then that, then I thought this and then felt that" and so on. Clients often answer our questions with an episodic and chronological account of what has transpired in the past. While these stories often provide interesting themes for further exploration, they sometimes waste time with extraneous information. Part of good facilitation is helping the coaching conversation focus on the important details and shift away from the irrelevant.

Asking for clarification—As a coach, you will experience moments when you are uncertain about what exactly the client means or to whom the client is referring. Perhaps the client uses an unclear pronoun or is talking about something complicated. Rather than letting them bull forward while you are unclear, just jump in and ask for clarification right away.

Seizing an important moment—From time to time, a client says something worth pouncing on in that exact moment. The immediacy of the moment can hold great emotional resonance and power. Maybe the client is talking about a lack of self-confidence and then, in midsentence, says, "I mean, I actually know I can do it." That is exactly the time the coach can jump in and say, "Wow! Did you hear what you just said?" This interjecting is perhaps superior to letting the client speak for another minute or two and then saying, "A couple of minutes ago you actually said that you believed you could do it."

Keeping track of time—Coaches are facilitators, and one of the basic skills of coaching is keeping track of time. We remain aware of the time available to us in the session, and we seek to use it as efficiently as possible with the session agenda in mind. Therefore, when clients go down verbal rabbit holes, deviate too far from the stated agenda, or risk running short on time, we may need to interrupt and redirect.

Looking at this short list, you will notice that the interruptions fall into two distinct categories. In his book *An Introduction to Coaching Skills*, Christian van Nieuwerburgh describes two types of "appropriate interruptions."[4] The first is a "procedural interruption," in which the interjection is offered to help manage the conversation. Timekeeping is an example of a procedural context in which interruption might be acceptable. The second category is "emphatic interruption," which happens in response to the risk that a critical moment might slip by unless the coach interjects. Highlighting an important point or celebrating a win are examples of occasions when emphatic interruptions might be well received.

I think of interruption as a technical skill that can be applied with greater or lesser degrees of grace. I typically interrupt in one of several ways that can be thought of on a continuum of politeness to rudeness (and I do them all from time to time). On the polite side of the spectrum, I might preface my interruption with a justification such as "With an eye on the clock, I'd like to jump in here" or "I'd like to jump in with a follow-up, if you don't mind." On the other end of the continuum, I just speak out forgoing niceties. I tend to do this specifically in the case of clarification or seizing on an important moment.

I also believe that interruption is stylistic. Some coaches will be more comfortable with this approach than others. Neither group is correct. Interrupters, like me, might occasionally plow over valuable information. By contrast, those who do not interrupt occasionally miss opportunities to seize upon golden moments. In the end, clients can be the final arbiter. If they do not mind the occasional interruption—and very few do when it is done well—then you have an additional arrow in your coaching quiver.

As a final consideration, I would ask that you reflect on your own tolerance of interruption. At first blush, you might say that you don't like to be interrupted. On deeper reflection, however, you will see that in many instances you do not mind it at all. When you fly, the captain sometimes interrupts your conversation to make a public announcement, and you aren't too angry about it. When an anxious woman holding a leash interrupts your lunch with a friend outside a café to ask, "Have you seen a little dog run by here?" you don't mind at all. When you say, "You know what?" and your witty friend offers a funny interjection before allowing you to continue, it's perfectly acceptable. What do all these examples have in common that allow these interruptions to be palatable? How can you re-create that in your own coaching?

REFLECT AND EXPERIMENT

- You probably do not like to be interrupted. List the assumptions you make about interruptions and interrupters. How many of these are always true, sometimes true, or rarely true?
- Pay attention to conversations in every area of your life. Pay particular attention to overlapping speech. Notice how often people interject a word or joke, laugh over a speaker, say "Mm-hmm," or give other types of interruptions. Notice how many of these are not disruptive to conversation and when they are occasionally disruptive.
- Try interrupting your clients. Yep. Do it strategically and kindly, but do it. See what effect it has on your client and your coaching.

Whose Language Is It, Anyway?

YOU'VE HEARD it many times: use the client's language. From coach training to master coaching, virtually everyone agrees that using the client's specific vocabulary when coaching is a wise move. If the client says "direct report," then you should adopt this phrase yourself. If, on the other hand, the client uses "supervisee," then it makes sense to adopt this word instead. If the client says "incensed" instead of "angry," then mimicking their unique language will be helpful. The rationale behind the use of client's language is multifaceted. The most common reasons I hear are as follows:

- *To demonstrate to the client that you are listening to them*—When the client says "incensed" instead of "angry," and you reflect that word back to them, they know you have heard them and are paying attention. The rationale here is that using the client's language is good for the coaching relationship. If the client calls their boss a "jerk," then it can become almost an inside joke if you ask about "the jerk."
- *To use terms with which the client is familiar and thereby put them at ease*—Every industry has its own vocabulary. If you

are engaged in any type of business coaching, then using words such as "KPIs," "line manager," and "strategy" will be familiar to the client. As a psychologist, I must be careful not to assume that my clients will understand my professional jargon. I avoid phrases such as "misattribution of arousal" and "high need for cognition" in favor of my client's vocabulary. Following your client's lead linguistically is a sure way to know that you are covering familiar ground and avoiding terms they might be self-conscious in admitting they do not know.

- *To avoid the trap of assuming you know what they mean*— Often, clients use language that suggests something, but we cannot be certain exactly what they mean. If they say there was a "situation at work," we assume a negative connotation but don't know much more than that. Using the word "situation" helps prevent too much interpretation on the coach's behalf.

The Client's Language or a Shared Language?

A subtle but important difference exists between the client's language and a shared language. If a major rationale for using the client's language is to enhance the coach-client relationship, then creating a shared language might be a superior strategy. This rarely emerges solely as a result of the coach parroting the client's language. Instead, it comes about when the conversation is co-created: when one person finishes another's sentence, when each person can anticipate what the other is going to say, when both people have the same idea at the same time ("I was just thinking the same thing!"), or when each person shares the same emotional experience. In one study, the researchers discovered that conversation partners who experienced a high degree of shared reality felt closer to one another and felt more certain of their perceptions.[1]

When We Might Use Coach Language

I have always wondered why we are encouraged to adopt the client's language without more serious thought given to when using the client's language is helpful and when using our own language is helpful. I first started thinking about this when I was interacting with my British colleagues. If they would use a particular Britishism, such as saying "lorry," "rucksack," or "barrister," I could appreciate their language but would not want to mimic it. If I said "rucksack," instead of the American alternative "backpack," it would sound inauthentic on my tongue. I realized that while I largely agree with using distinctive bits of a client's language, it is also important to use one's own authentic language.

Ultimately, I found two examples of places in coaching where I think the adage "Use the client's language" does not always apply. I began experimenting with methods for creating a shared language and have experienced some powerful moments in my coaching sessions as a result. The two areas are metaphors and strengths splitting.

Metaphor

In 2005, I attended the annual conference of the International Coaching Federation in San Jose, California, where Cynthia Darst presented a wonderful workshop on using metaphor in coaching. One of the activities involved us writing a phrase on a piece of paper and then using it later as a metaphor in our partner coaching. The papers included phrases such as "a dog chasing its tail" and "being late for the bus" and "making a smoothie in a blender." What I found so interesting was that we did not have to wait for the client to offer a metaphor. These randomly generated metaphors worked well.

Since that conference in 2005, I have been paying attention to the frequency with which metaphors emerge from my clients' language versus those that I offer. We use them approximately equally, and I cannot discern any difference in effectiveness between the two. At times, my client will say something like "My back is against a wall," and we will just go with that as a metaphor. At other times, I might offer an image of my own, such as "It sounds like you are walking on a tightrope." I cannot recall a single instance in which a client was taken aback that I offered a metaphor of my own construction. A few times, the client immediately modified my metaphor, saying, for example, "Yes, but in this tightrope act, there is no safety net."

I have come to believe that coach-driven metaphors are as effective as they are because they create a shared reality for the coach and client to explore. When the client is discussing an actual problem, their mental model of the issue will necessarily differ from that of the coach. As soon as the pair begin constructing a metaphor to represent the problem, though, they are truly co-creating a shared understanding of the issue.

Strengths Spotting

Strengths spotting, as the name suggests, is identifying a client's strengths. Many coaches do this with the aid of a formal strengths assessment such as the CliftonStrengths assessment or the Strengths Profile. Strengths spotting, by contrast, is an informal method of identifying strengths as you hear your clients express excitement about areas of high proficiency. This technique offers a way of introducing strengths labels into the coaching conversation so that you and your client might discuss how, when, and with whom they might use their strength.

Standard coaching wisdom would tell us that the best way to find a client's strengths is to simply ask the question, "What are your strengths?" This, I believe, is ill-advised for many reasons. The principal drawback is that the answer relies solely on your client's strengths vocabulary. If your client knows only a handful of strengths labels, that will limit your conversation. Not only that, but the answer will provide little new information or insight for your client. "What are your strengths?" turns out to be a question that primarily serves the coach.

I like to weigh in with a strengths label of my own. I know! This flies in the face of the adage that we should not label others as well as the adage that we use the client's language. The upside of this technique is that it opens the door to better co-creation and a shared reality and can pinpoint a wider range of strengths. I once said, for example, "You seem like you love to solve puzzles. I can see how excited you are by putting all the pieces in place. I am curious if we might be looking at a strength called *puzzler*?" In fact, my client responded to that comment with enthusiasm, telling me that she often did puzzles at home, was excellent at solving problems, and loved having such a unique label.

I treat these labels like tentative hypotheses. I offer them to my clients but am happy to change course if my client rejects the label. I am also happy to say to my client, "Well, you seem to think it's a strength, but you don't love the word *puzzler*. What might you call it instead?" The client is then fully empowered to bring her own language to the table but has also benefited from my relatively large strengths vocabulary.

Conclusion

In the end, I actually agree with the idea that we should largely notice and reflect our client's language. This advice has endured because of its general benefits. Even so, I feel that many coaches develop an orthodox view of this topic that limits them from the potential benefit of alternative approaches. Pondering the potential benefits of coach-directed language might lead to more flexible coaching practices. Similarly, paying attention to shared language and under-standing—rather than just the client's language—might have payoffs for the coaching alliance.

REFLECT AND EXPERIMENT

- Pay attention to your own practice. How often in a session do you note and reflect a unique piece of your client's vocabulary? How is it that you decided to focus on that particular terminology rather than other things your client said? What do you think the benefits of this standard practice are?
- Try offering a metaphor of your own based on your professional intuition and your existing knowledge of your client. Pay particular attention to how your client reacts and how useful the metaphor intervention is.
- Consider your penchant for reframing. Coaches often reframe client statements in ways that bring a fresh perspective. If you do this, consider the extent to which this technique is an example of using your own language. In what other areas do you think it might be permissible or beneficial to use the coach's language?

What Are Symmetries in Questioning?

POWERFUL QUESTIONS are, in many ways, the heart of coaching. People who have gone through formal coach training know that coaching is an inquiry-based endeavor. It works best when coaches ask curious questions—preferably, questions that the clients have not thought to ask themselves. The measure of the value of coaching is the extent to which the client has an opportunity not just for reflection but for *novel* reflection.

We all know the basic architecture of so-called powerful questions: they tend to be short and open-ended and provoke reflection. Fair enough. I believe we can also look at questions with a greater degree of sophistication. For example, are there distinct types of powerful questions? Table 10.1 shows one framework for addressing this question that I arrived at in collaboration with a group of health coaches.

Each of these types of questions might be useful to the extent that each offers clients a new avenue for reflection. How do we know which questions clients have already asked themselves, and which will be the most provocative for them? In short, we do not

TABLE 10.1. Types of coaching questions

Type	Definition	Examples
Evergreen	General questions that can be used multiple times with a client and across multiple situations	What do you value? What's next? What are you learning about this?
Solutions-focused	Questions focused on achieving a desirable outcome	What do you want? What would you prefer? When have you successfully dealt with something similar in the past?
Problem-focused	Questions focused on managing or removing undesirable obstacles	What's holding you back? What are you afraid of? What's standing in your way?
One-time or occasional use	Unusual questions that might lose power if asked multiple times	If your health could speak, what would it say to you? How might you best use your strength of puzzler here?

know. This is why we ask a number of questions and explore a variety of themes and angles during a session. When I train coaches, I often say, "Not every question needs to be a bull's-eye. Typically, clients feel that a session was valuable if two or three questions provide a new insight." I'd love to see research done on this. What is the typical number of questions that yield powerful results? My hunch is that, if expressed as a ratio, it would be about one or two out of fifteen.

Theory of Mind and Coaching Questions

The ability to ask great questions—if we define those, in part, as questions that have not previously occurred to the client—rests on the concept psychologists call *theory of mind*.[1] Theory of mind describes the ability to make reasonable guesses about another person's state of mind. If you tell me that you were in a car accident, I don't smile and say, "Congratulations!" because I understand that the ordeal was likely stressful and scary for you. When I see my client sigh deeply as they talk about their plan, I can make a reasonable guess that they are experiencing some unpleasant emotions or uncertainty.

Theory of mind also extends to making careful assumptions about what another person knows. When I show up to the post office, for instance, I never have to ask, "Do you speak English with proficiency?" because I understand that English is a basic mandate for a postal job in my country. Similarly, I don't have to explain or describe ice cream to an adult friend because I can guess that they already understand the concept of ice cream. On the other hand, I might ask someone if they have a background in statistics before assuming that they know concepts such as platykurtic or stochastic distributions.

The same holds true with our coaching clients. I am often tempted to ask questions of my client and then realize that my client likely already knows the answer. For example, if my client is considering whether to accept a new job, I might be tempted to ask, "What are the pros and cons of the new job?" Using theory of mind, however, I know that my client has almost certainly gone down the rabbit hole of pros and cons long before they showed up to our coaching session.

At last, we have arrived at the concept of symmetries and asymmetries in coaching questions: the idea that various matches or mismatches can exist between what the client knows and what the coach knows.

Symmetries and Asymmetries in Coaching Questions

I understand that none of us can truly know what another person knows. When I suggest that a coach knows what the client is thinking or knows how the client will answer a question, I mean that they have an extremely educated guess with a high likelihood of accuracy. With that said, I think that either the coach or the client knows the answer to certain questions as well as neither or both. Take a look at table 10.2 to better understand this framework. It describes the knowledge of the coach and the client at the moment the question is asked.

In my experience, questions from the top row are not very useful. Admittedly, I don't see many rhetorical questions asked. By contrast, I often see advice offered disguised as a question. This happens, I believe, because coaches sometimes have an insight about the client

TABLE 10.2. Symmetries and asymmetries in coaching questions

	The client knows the answer	The client does not know the answer
The coach knows the answer	Rhetorical questions: "Do you want to get fired?"	Advice disguised as a question: "How would it be for you to directly ask your supervisor for more responsibility?"
The coach does not know the answer	Clarifying questions: "What do you mean by 'a mess'?" Questions inducing an emotional state: "How did your team react to your winning the award?"	Powerful questions: "What has been your best management experience to date?" "What are the most important elements of your vision?"

and can see something that would potentially help the client. Unfortunately, advice-laden questions often narrow the coach's focus. I have seen even intermediate-level coaches get stuck trying to convince their clients that a particular course of action is recommended. I know they know better than to do this, but since the advice comes in the Trojan horse of the question format, perhaps it appears more allowable.

The bottom row of the table is where the best questions are because they are questions to which the client does not immediately know the answer. These queries are an invitation to reflect and thereby gain new insight. The powerful questions are those that the client needs to reflect on to answer, and the coach has no real idea of where the answer might be. If I ask clients, "What is the most important learning you are taking from today's session?" I have no idea what they might say, and they must do some mental digging to identify and articulate an answer.

Creating this simple table helped me understand something about questions. In some instances—shown in the lower left—the client already has an answer ready that can still be useful to the coaching process. The two instances I have identified where this can occur are in the cases of clarifying questions and mood induction questions. I use these judiciously, but I do use them.

In the end, I have found it useful to think in terms of theory of mind and symmetries in my coaching questions. I understand that my best questions—those that my clients respond to with "That's a good question"—are those for which I don't have any guesses as to how the client might answer.

REFLECT AND EXPERIMENT

- Pay attention to your own coaching questions. Use a continuum that ranges from one to ten along which you guess the client's answer. Let one be "I have absolutely no idea whatsoever," let five be "I generally think they will go this direction, but I am not certain of the specifics," and let ten be "I am confident I can predict exactly what my client will say." Undoubtedly, your questions will vary along this continuum. Try tracking your questions, rating them, and seeing which types yield the best results.

- Be mindful of the strategic uses of questions the client already knows the answer to. In some instances, a little clarification for the coach can streamline the overall process. Similarly, other times we intentionally ask the client to recount a story—even though they already know the details—because of the effect this might have on their confidence or mood.

- Try your hand at categorizing types of questions. Consider testing these questions with a colleague or client. Create your own framework, and see what insights might emerge from the process.

Why Do We Need More Small Talk in Coaching?

WHEN I train coaches—whether they are people new to the profession who want to set up a private practice or managers who want to learn coaching skills—I notice a common reticence around powerful questions. Many people seem reluctant to ask questions that are too big, too personal, or too challenging. Their instinct is that such questions might be upsetting or intimidating to their clients. What I notice is that people with this mindset typically want to slowly warm up to the big important questions. The truth is, I don't think this is necessary. I think a contract exists between coach and client that allows coaches to ask deep, probing, and challenging questions. I think, however, that something sensible lies in the heart of the intuitions of beginners. I view it as a "small talk" attitude because it so closely resembles the politeness of everyday speech. When we meet someone for the first time—at a party, on a plane, or at a dinner— we confine our topics of conversation to relatively tame scripts. We might ask, "What do you do for a living?" or "What brought you to this part of the country?" These conversational protocols allow us to connect without too much intimacy or the threat of causing too much offense. Imagine, by contrast, if you turned to the person in the seat beside you on an airplane and asked, "What are you most afraid of?" or "Who is the ideal you?" They would probably request a change of seat! Everyday interactions—especially among strangers and acquaintances—follow a norm of politeness.

I argue here that no such norm exists in coaching nor should it. By following the route of so-called small talk, many coaches slow down the coaching process unnecessarily and limit the potential power of coaching conversations.

Depth- versus Surface-Level Coaching

I like to distinguish between depth- and surface-level coaching. Many experienced coaches who are reading this might think, "Sure, so do I. We should coach depth," which is certainly an understandable viewpoint. However, I might mean something mildly different when I refer to depth-level coaching. Surface-level coaching, to me, focuses on practical matters. It includes the who, when, and where questions. This method is the small talk of coaching because questions such as "Who can help you?" and "When might you start on this?" are fairly nonthreatening. Surface-level coaching is a vital part of the coaching process as it is concrete, fast-paced, and results focused.

Regardless of your style or type of coaching, you will notice that sessions tend to start and end at the surface level. When we set an agenda for the session, we ask practical questions such as "What would you like to focus on?" and "What would be a successful session for you?" As our time together wraps up, we move to the surface again with questions such as "What have you learned in this session?" "What will you do to apply this learning?" and "When will you do that?" Surface-level coaching offers the sigh of relief that social small talk does.

By contrast, much of the middle portion of our coaching sessions is conducted at the depth level. Depth questions—or "big talk" questions—typically include those starting with *how* or *why*. They focus on critical client processes and values. They are insight focused rather than action focused, and they do in fact require a little more time and trust. Table 11.1 includes more differences.

My provocation is this: less experienced coaches seem to struggle more with big-talk questions, and more experienced coaches seem inclined to prefer big-talk over small-talk questions.

A Flexible Use of Big and Small Talk

Let's return to our metaphor of meeting someone new at a dinner party. We feel safe to ask predictable small-talk questions such as "What part of town do you live in?" "Where do you work?" and "Where did you grow up?" This allows the relationship to slowly warm up without too many opportunities for offense. Imagine, by contrast, that you asked your new acquaintance, "What have you been learning recently?" "What's most important to you?" or "What do you do that you find most fulfilling?" Sure, your conversation partner might furrow their brow as they see you wander off script, but they will likely respond well. These questions matter and can facilitate a greater degree of intimacy without prying too deeply into a person's most sensitive or vulnerable areas. I have experimented with this many times over the years, and it mostly fast-forwards connection in a powerful way.

TABLE 11.1. Surface- and depth-level questions in coaching

Mode	Questions	Benefits	Limitations
Surface	Who When Where	Fast-paced Concrete Nonthreatening Results focused	Situationally specific Shallow
Depth	How Why	Process oriented Broadly applicable Insight focused	Trust required Slower pace

The drawback to these powerful questions is that they can be too powerful. I was once coached by someone who was skilled at asking such questions. Over the course of our session, I felt as if I was being shelled by an enemy: "What do you value?" "What's holding you back?" "What's most important right now?" "How do you prioritize?" and the list went on. I was almost breathless in the barrage of deep coaching. Simply put, I needed to come up for air. A few practical questions such as "How might you use this insight?" or "What about this feels like something you can apply?" would have worked wonders for me.

In the end, I think it makes sense—even for coaches with years of experience—to reflect on the relative ratio of big and small questions, the practical, result-oriented inquiries versus queries that are deep and provocative. Similarly, try creating a map of your sessions and consider where exactly you are asking your deepest questions and where you are asking about practical matters. Most importantly, pay particular attention to your clients' reactions to both types of questions, and consider adapting your coaching accordingly.

REFLECT AND EXPERIMENT

- We all know the advantages in coaching the person and not the problem. The client is of course heavily attached to their own goals, but as coaches, we can focus more on processes rather than outcomes. Even so, it makes sense to notice if you have types of clients in terms of their preference for surface- versus depth-level coaching or if certain types of agendas lend themselves more readily to one or the other. It might be helpful if you made a table or chart in which you listed your clients' agendas and then created a matrix of surface- and depth-level questions and strategies that might address each. What do you notice?

- Experiment in your own coaching with periods of practical, fast, and nonthreatening questions. Note the pace of progress, your client's reactions, and your own experience.
- Play around with the beginning and end of your sessions. Are there ways that you can eek more out of your sessions by changing the ratio of so-called small and big questions at each end of your time with your client?
- Ask yourself, "Is this the provocation Robert changed his mind about?" (as he mentioned in the opening pages of this part of the book). Yes, it is.

What If We Didn't Say Anything at All?

NOT LONG ago, I observed a coaching session in which the coach—a person I knew to be brash and gregarious in everyday conversation—said very little. I was surprised not only by his reserve but also by how effective it was. He spoke only a few times throughout the session. As a result, the client went on, telling stories, venting, circling back, and going deeper. Although I value occasional and strategic silence, I know that I am often hesitant to be too silent because I want to facilitate in a way that keeps the coaching moving forward efficiently. In this instance, however, the silence seemed to allow the space for the client to really inhabit the coaching session, to feel heard, and to articulate difficult thoughts.

I left that observation thinking a great deal about the use of silence in coaching. As a thought experiment, I considered how little we might speak during a coaching session. Anchoring one end of the continuum would be a session in which the coach said absolutely nothing. My instinct is that such a session would be strange, anxiety provoking, and largely ineffective. At the other end of the continuum would be a session in which the coach speaks the entire time. It would be, for all intents and purposes, a lecture. The client might gain some benefit in this, but it wouldn't really be coaching. And then all the space in the middle exists as well.

All experienced coaches, I believe, have an appreciation of silence. Suggesting that coaches should occasionally use silence to benefit clients is not very provocative. What may be more provocative is to suggest that we don't know all that much about how silence is used, when it occurs, and what the benefits and drawbacks of its use in coaching are. I often hear coaches describe silence as if it is a single monolithic tool, such as observing a shift in the client or using a metaphor. What follows is a meditation on silence in coaching that, I hope, provokes new thinking and engagement with the topic.

A Deeper Look at Silence

Let's begin by examining the concept of silence itself before we talk about its application to coaching. My first inkling that we need to reflect on the fundamental question of what silence is came when I started carefully observing coaching sessions. I noticed that silence came in all shapes and sizes: pauses when a client was trying to think of a word, breaks between the coach's and the client's turn to speak, protracted periods of quiet in which the client reflected, and moments of uncertainty where the conversation just seemed to grind to a temporary halt. This dovetails with the lay understanding of silence in everyday conversation. We have "pregnant pauses," "companionable silences," "stony silences," "codes of silence," and the ironic "deafening silence," and we can give someone "the silent treatment." Each of these phrases denotes a silence of unique quality. I noticed, in essence, that silence is a many-splendored thing. It involves far more than the coach choosing to be quiet.

Some people say that silence isn't nothing; it is something. This quip is not just clever wordplay but also a profound observation. Although we could be tempted to think of silence as the absence of speech, silence is more than verbal negative space. Because coaching is, at its heart, a conversational technology, I love that the linguist Michal Ephratt refers to silence as eloquent.[1] It serves its own communicative purposes. To understand those purposes, I turned to research in linguistics, where researchers have been studying silence for about fifty years.

Among the seminal writings on the topic was Vernon Jensen's paper that identified distinct purposes of intentional silence.[2] In my own words, these include the following attributes:

- *Linking*—A shared moment of silence can be just that, a shared experience. In this way, silence can connect people. An example of this can be seen in Israeli society, on Yom HaShoah, the day that commemorates the millions murdered in the Holocaust. On that day, air raid sirens blast for two minutes, and the nation grinds to a silent halt. People pull over their cars on the freeways, come to a halt on the sidewalk, and otherwise make collective space for this important moment.
- *Affecting*—Typically, this refers to being cold or unresponsive and putting on an affectation of silence to communicate to a speaker that you are in disagreement or are uninterested.
- *Revelational*—In this instance, silence can reveal that a person doesn't know enough to have something to say. A student, for instance, might stay largely silent in favor of a lecture from the more knowledgeable instructor.
- *Activating*—All people, including coaches and clients, sometimes stop talking for a moment to choose their words carefully.

Each of these purposes relates thematically to coaching: making room, sharing an experience, communicating a personal stance, adopting a beginner's mind, and articulating one's inner experience are all critical aspects of coaching, and all are embedded in silence.

Silence in Coaching

In 2014, Annette Fillery-Travis and Elaine Cox presented a linguistic continuum of coaching.[3] At one end, they marked interactions that were "linguistically rich," such as asking questions. More linguistically neutral interactions included paraphrasing of nonverbal communication. At the other end were the linguistically poor (but no less powerful) interactions, such as listening, silence, and thinking. One aspect of mature professional intuition might be the ability to intentionally switch between styles of linguistic richness—that is, to know when to speak and when to shut up.

We can begin to explore this idea, in part, by looking at research from clinical psychology. In 2003, three psychologists published a survey of therapist attitudes toward silence in sessions.[4] They discovered that—like coaches—therapists were extraordinarily comfortable with using silence and believed that they had become more comfortable with silence across the course of their careers. In addition, the research participants highly agreed that silence was useful for (1) observing the client, (2) conveying interest to the client, and (3) focusing on what is going on with the client. This suggests that our professional cousins have intuitions about silence that are not dissimilar from our own.

David Drake, the pioneer of narrative coaching, once said, in essence, that coaches should not speak unless what they are going to say is going to be more powerful than silence. This reinforces the weight, importance, and usefulness that we place on silence in coaching. David suggests that silence in coaching is a clear demonstration that the coach is willing to receive whatever the client is articulating. It conveys a trust in both the client and the coaching process itself. David writes, "In this sense, silence is both an inner state and an outer stance."[5]

David's thoughts on silence in coaching led me to review what other thought leaders have to say on the topic. Across two dozen thinkers, here are some of the most consistent and interesting points that have emerged:

- *Make space for client reflection*—This can be seen not only in being quiet but also in remaining silent, at times, even after clients have finished speaking. Occasionally, this additional silence allows them to pick back up and explore further.
- *Make space for personal observation*—When coaches remain silent, including quieting the narrative that may be running in their own mind, they free themselves up to notice more about their clients.
- *Pressure the client to take responsibility for reflection*—Because experienced coaches, like therapists, tend to be comfortable with silence, we are generally more capable of tolerating the awkwardness of silence than our clients are. As a result, if we choose to remain silent, it shifts the responsibility for speaking to our clients. This can be particularly useful in instances when clients might rush to closure on questions by simply saying, "I don't know."
- *Build the relationship*—Because silence is an aspect of excellent listening, strategic silence from the coach can demonstrate to clients that we are interested in what they have to say and are respectful of their process of reflection and articulation. This, in turn, enhances the coaching alliance.
- *Building the capacity to sit*—A lesser discussed aspect of silence is that it offers clients an opportunity to slow down and think things through carefully. In a fast-paced world, coaching can be thought of as *slow time,* and silence is a major component of this.
- *Listen for thematic silence*—Coaches can listen to what is not being said (a form of thematic silence) as well as what is being described. This instance of silence is on behalf of the client rather than the coach.

The more I read the research and theory on silence and the more conversations I had with other coaches on this topic, the more I saw that we are only beginning to scratch the surface of our understanding. I find this exciting rather than daunting because having new ideas about coaching keeps me engaged with the practice and helps me to serve my clients better.

REFLECT AND EXPERIMENT

- How comfortable are you with silence? Perhaps give yourself a rating from one to ten. Has it always been like this, or have you noticed changes over the course of your coaching career? If so, what factors have helped you become more comfortable with silence?

- Consider recording one of your coaching sessions: pay attention to the number of times you speak, how long you speak for each time, and how long the silences go. What do you make of this?

- How comfortable are you with the idea that you can use silence to strategically pressure your client to take greater responsibility in a session? If you see an appropriate opportunity to do so, try it out. See how you and your client react.

- Consider the continuum of linguistically rich and poor interactions, bearing in mind that *poor* simply means not a lot of language is occurring. What would you guess is the ratio in your typical session? What might be the pros and cons of changing this ratio?

- Experiment with saying less. Find ways to allow silence to unfold a little longer than you normally might. Perhaps suggest to your client that they sit with a question before answering it right away. What do you notice?

PART THREE
Common Coaching Concepts

C OACHING has a global culture based on standard practices, mindsets, and an appreciation of common concepts. Coaches of all stripes, for instance, think that curiosity is integral to the coaching process in a way that it might not be for golf course groundskeepers or construction flaggers (those fields have their own strengths and emphases). Coaches are familiar with the way curiosity can fuel strong questions. In fact, curiosity is specifically mentioned in two of the core competencies of the International Coaching Federation. Similarly, all coaches will be familiar with so-called aha moments. These concepts—and the specific language that accompanies them—are part of what gives rise to a coherent professional culture and sense of cohesion for coaches working in widely different industries and cultures.

This part addresses some of the most common coaching concepts. It begins by inviting you to consider the concept of observation. Coaches tend to be keen observers, noticing even subtle shifts in mood, posture, and language. Even so, coaches might have room to grow when it comes to observing other people coach. We can be strongly tempted to attend to an inner monologue about how we would coach this client rather than learning from what another coach is doing.

From here, the provocations veer from the thought-provoking questions of wondering whether we can trust our clients' eureka moments to how much curiosity we should employ to whether we might be more effective if we used less, rather than more, empathy. Two other provocations round out this part. First, we rethink the age-old habit of discouraging our assumptions—maybe making assumptions is useful. The part then closes with a musing about the role of self-disclosure in coaching.

The provocations in this book vary to the degree to which they will challenge readers. Some, such as the encouragement to interrupt more, are likely more challenging to readers than the suggestion that coaches could benefit from studying learning theory. Be forewarned: this part contains two provocations—can we trust aha moments and what if we used less empathy—that likely lean toward the challenging side of the spectrum. As always, make up your own mind after you have had an opportunity to discuss and experiment with the concepts in your own coaching.

Why Aren't We Better at Observing Coaching?

ALMOST EVERY day, I go for a walk in my neighborhood. I pass by many wooden poles that hold aloft the wires that provide phone and internet services and power to my area. The vast majority of the time, I don't even notice them. Occasionally, such as the time an owl landed on one or the time a person was repairing one, I look up and take note of the poles and lines. They seem to include jumbles of wires that snake out from square or round metal boxes. I notice that some of the lines are higher and some are lower. Over time, I became curious about what I was seeing, and I chose to learn more about them. It turns out, the tallest wires carry high-voltage electricity, midlevel wires carry lower voltage, and the lowest wires are telephone and cable. The boxes are transformers that convert the high voltage to a lower voltage more appropriate to power a home. Finally, the cylinders that look sort of like springs are to protect the poles from lightning strikes. Now, when I take my walks, I find that I look more often at the poles, understand them better, and appreciate the subtle differences between them.

This raises the old adage about the difference between looking and truly seeing. We can view observation as existing on a continuum that stretches from not noticing to noticing to carefully noticing to truly appreciating. My own coaching improved dramatically when I started using this framework to observe myself at work. For a long time, I labored under the assumption that my coaching would improve most from practice. I largely overlooked the gains to be had from observing the coaching of others. In fact, observation as a tool for improvement exists in all areas of my life: my rock climbing improved when I paid attention to the techniques of better climbers, and my drawing got better when I looked at what professional artists were doing.

Fortunately, we have ample opportunities to observe coaching. Training inevitably includes coaching demonstrations. You can join mentoring or supervision groups, watch demonstrations at professional meetings and conferences, and participate in roundtable coaching groups and public online demonstrations. If I had to guess, I would estimate that I observe twenty to thirty coaching sessions a year outside of the work I do as a mentor coach and supervisor.

For some readers, this thought will be stimulating. Like me, you might have overlooked opportunities to observe coaching as a means of professional development. For other readers, you will have arrived at this conclusion independently of me. Even so, I would ask you, "What you are doing to improve not just your coaching but your observational skills? Do you ever reflect on your ability to observe? To what extent are you aware of aspects of observation that come naturally to you and others that might be areas of weakness? Do you ask yourself what exactly you are observing for?"

Obstacles to Deep Observation

If observing coaching were easy, we would all do it in the most masterful way possible. I know that this is not the case because I have improved greatly at this skill over the years. Unless every other coach is just naturally better at observation than I am, I assume all coaches could improve at this with effort. This line of thinking had me wondering about the following common obstacles to deep observation.

Coaching Instead of Observing

I am certain that readers will smile in familiarity with this particular obstacle. Not silently coaching along with the person who is actively coaching can be exceedingly difficult. As observers, we can see a wide field just as coaches can sometimes see a broader landscape than our clients can. We might be tempted to pay attention to the client rather than the coach. This leads us to mentally yell, "The client is handing you a metaphor! Use the metaphor!" or "Wow, you just missed an opportunity to ask about a seemingly critical theme." When we engage in this mental coaching, we aren't observing, we are participating. Even worse, we aren't learning because we are only ever going to coach the way we coach. Nothing new is happening.

Getting Distracted

The mind is a busy place—more like a bustling Turkish market than a peaceful English library. Second to second, we are making judgments and decisions, interpreting and anticipating, analyzing and disagreeing, making inferences, and the list goes on. Add to this mental chatter the incoming text messages, the activity happening outside our windows, and the soft rubbing of your kitty along your leg, and it's a wonder you know what is happening at all.

Being Wedded to Our Own Tools

Sometimes, coaches can get wrapped up in their own tools and frameworks. When coaches are fascinated by concepts such as the mind-body connection, clean language, or self-compassion, they might be tempted to use this idea as a lens through which to observe another person's coaching. Unfortunately, this can limit learning because it prevents the observer from being exposed to new tools and frameworks and their potential benefits.

Being Overly Positive

Many public coaching sessions I have observed have been followed by what I would consider to be fairly superficial debriefing conversations. The audience crows about how amazing the coaching was, the facilitator gushes about the session, and the coach weighs in with sage-like wisdom. Fair enough, but I fear people might miss an opportunity to discuss the coaching in full. What about the moments that didn't go well or seemed difficult or puzzling?

To illustrate this last point, here is an example from a recent public coaching session I observed. At the conclusion of the session, the coach asked the client to articulate what she was walking away with. Here, to the best of my recollection, is the transcript of that interaction:

Coach: What are you walking away with from today's session?

Client: The practical thing I am walking away with—and I am really excited to have something practical—is that I can hire someone to help me with this issue. I don't know why I didn't think of that before!

Coach: Does it matter?

Client: What?

Coach: Does it matter why you didn't think of it before?

Client: Uh, no, I guess not.

As I observed this, the interaction felt like a failure of coaching presence. Here the client was expressing her enthusiasm, and rather than acknowledging the excitement, the coach chose to challenge the client. The challenge appeared frivolous to me as it didn't result in a major insight, nor would we expect it to. Frankly, it seemed like an odd choice at the end of a session. It made me wonder if coaches have one mindset in the middle of a session, where exploration, challenge, and planning are more common, and another at the end of the session, which is typically marked by learning capture, celebration, and accountability. If nothing else, I learned from the session by thinking more articulately about this across-session shift in the coaching mindset.

I was curious about the coach's rationale for the challenge, and I was interested in the client's experience as well. The client appeared to benefit from the coaching and seemingly wasn't taken aback too much by this stylistic choice. My instinct is that the positivity of coaching culture blocks our ability to discuss these types of issues. I would have loved to have heard the coach say, "Oh yeah, I made a mistake there" or "Even though that might have been a mistake, I don't think it matters because small blunders don't impact coaching effectiveness as much as we might think." Either comment would have led to a more fruitful conversation than the audience marveling at how great the coach was.

What Are We Observing For?

The single question that most enhanced my ability to deeply interface with the coaching sessions I observed was "What am I looking for?" By this, I meant to challenge myself to consider what my own objectives were in the process of observation. For instance, when I act in the role of mentor or supervisor, I am often looking for demonstrations of basic competence with beginning coaches or professional maturity with intermediate coaches. This singular way to observe is a clipboard-in-hand approach, where I am keeping an eye out for a specific set of themes and skills and mentally ticking them when I see them.

The supervisory lens is different from when I observe to learn. In this latter case, I keep an eye out for some distinct themes and outcomes. These motifs include the following:

- *Observing for inspiration*—Perhaps my favorite aspect of observing coaching is witnessing stylistic differences. I love the fact that people coach differently from the way I do. I have learned a great deal from coaches who hardly say anything, never interrupt or take risks with what is appropriate in coaching. For instance, I once observed a coach do a Google search in the middle of the session and share the results with their client to get their client's reaction—not exactly something they teach in coach training programs, but it worked surprisingly well in this specific instance.

- *Observing to hone noticing skills*—In addition to observing to enhance my own coaching skills, I observe to hone my noticing skills. I am focused heavily on the coach side of the conversation, but I also attend to the client so I see what the coach is reacting to. I am paying attention to the client's language, emotional expression, and themes they are discussing. On the coach side of the equation, I am noticing pace, verbal fluency, word choice, attention, empathy, humor, flexibility, note-taking, and many other factors.

- *Observing for interesting moments*—I will conclude with the single most profound shift in my ability to observe coaching. I used to look for a display of skills or the nature of the relationship. Now I focus most heavily on *interesting moments*—not critical moments, such as those that lead to flashes of insight (although they might be these). Instead, I am happy to see any moment that captures my curiosity. It might be an unusually long period of silence, an instance where the coach isn't certain where to head or the client's correction of a specific word, or a sudden shift in the stated agenda. I've noticed that keeping an eye out for interesting moments gets me out of my own head and shifts me out of "coach mode" so I can see what is unfolding before me.

REFLECT AND EXPERIMENT

- How often do you observe the coaching of your colleagues? Take time to research ways that you might up the ante on your observations.
- Consider writing or otherwise articulating a specific agenda for your observations. This might be something such as "I am going to take away two stylistic differences from this coach to consider in my own coaching" or "I am going to try to identify the most unexpected questions the coach asks." Note the effect that doing this has on your ability to observe carefully.
- One person you can observe is yourself. With your client's permission, consider recording a session now, and play it back so that you can see yourself coach.

PROVOCATION 14

Can We Trust Eureka Moments?

AS COACHES, we are exceedingly familiar with the flashes of insight that clients experience as a result of our powerful questions. These moments typically feel great to the client and pretty good to us as well. In fact, these flashes are so common in, and so central to, good coaching that I would bet many coaches see them as a crucial outcome of the coaching endeavor.

Traditionally, these moments have been labeled *eureka moments*. This Greek word is a reference to Archimedes, the ancient Greek mathematician who laid down much of the foundation for modern physics. The classic story says that Archimedes stepped into a bathtub and noticed that the water rose upward in direct proportion to the amount of the body part—his leg—he submerged in the bath. What you and I might think of as a mild parlor trick of physical action and reaction was the core of Archimedes's principle (the idea that the relative density of an object can be measured through water displacement). My favorite part of the story—surely apocryphal— is that Archimedes then ran through the streets naked, shouting, "Eureka!" (I found it!).

Our clients' insights might not always be as consequential as that of Archimedes, and they hopefully won't run from our sessions naked, but those moments are still terrific. In fact, we place an unusually high premium on them when we ask, "What insights have you gained in this session?" and "How might you apply those insights?" I am not going to argue that this tactic is wrong. I put stock in aha moments the same as any other coach. Instead, this provocation is aimed at digging a little deeper into the phenomenon of insight so that we might be able to relate to it in more sophisticated ways.

Insight as a Coaching Outcome

Years ago, the late Anthony Grant—the pioneer of coaching psychology—articulated a number of methodological limitations of using return on investment as an outcome measure of coaching success.[1] I would add to his litany of complaints that because so many other factors impact bottom-line success at work, drawing a direct link between coaching and those outcomes is difficult. Tony advocated for a "well-being and engagement" approach to evaluating coaching. Much in the same way that well-being metrics can serve to augment traditional economic measures, such as gross domestic product, well-being can provide a lens to evaluate coaching.

This idea has been echoed by a number of other coaching researchers. Tia Moin and Christian van Nieuwerburgh, for instance, conducted research to better understand clients' experience of positive psychology coaching and discovered that clients felt more self-aware, motivated, and self-efficacious.[2] Similarly, Cornelia Lucey and van Nieuwerburgh found that clients experienced increases in positive emotions and self-compassion.[3] In a third study, Alexandra Fouracres and van Nieuwerburgh discovered that clients who engage in discussions about their strengths find the events positive and enjoy boosts in authenticity.[4] Taken together, these studies suggest that client variables, rather than work outcomes, are a more fruitful way to understand the value of coaching.

This brings us to an interesting issue: the question of what exactly clients consider to be a coaching success. Is it related to their progress on goals? To the pace of that progress? To explore these questions, Leticia Mosteo and her colleagues collected data from nearly two hundred bank executives who participated in coaching. The research team discovered that 72 percent of the participants identified self-awareness as a key value of coaching.[5] This statistic is interesting. Although clients come to coaching with specific goals and problems in mind, personal insight and self-awareness are the currencies of coaching once it starts.

Let me put this in the boldest way I know how: clients are typically satisfied with sessions if they experience a flash of insight or otherwise gain a bit of self-knowledge. They don't even need to have much of it. One or two insights, in my experience, and the session is a success for the client. To me, this issue is a prickly one because on one hand, I want to honor the client's values and experience, but on the other hand, I know we can do better than insight. Let's take a look.

Understanding Flashes of Insight

We all have personal experience with flashes of insight. These are ideas that suddenly pop into mind and offer either a fresh perspective or a perceived solution to our problem. We can experience them in mundane ways, such as suddenly knowing the answer to a riddle (Question: Which month has twenty-eight days? Answer: All of them!). We also experience them in profound ways, such as clients who suddenly realize that a solution is right in front of them or that making a major change is much easier than they had anticipated.

Researchers Amory Danek and Jennifer Wiley have identified a number of characteristics that consistently define these eureka moments.[6] These include the following:

- *Suddenness*—Flashes of insight appear all at once rather than incrementally.
- *Surprise*—Because they appear all at once, they can feel surprising.
- *Certainty*—People typically sense that the insight is true and definitive.
- *Pleasure*—People experience some range of pleasurable emotions, such as relief.
- *Drive*—The insight seems to increase engagement, motivation, and optimism.

Other researchers have weighed in on a critical aspect of aha moments: the certainty that surrounds them. Sascha Topolinski and Rolf Reber, for instance, argue that when information comes to mind easily, we have more confidence in it.[7] For instance, if I were to ask you when your birthday is, you would be able to easily tell me and to do so with confidence. If, on the other hand, I were to ask you the date of your parents' wedding anniversary, you might still be able to tell me, but your answer would require marginally more thought, and your confidence would be incrementally less than the certainty you have regarding your own birthday. The researchers also argue that the positive emotions that come with flashes of insight serve as cues to make the insights feel true.

Building on these ideas, Ruben Laukkonen and his colleagues propose that people have a eureka heuristic.[8] Heuristics are mental shortcuts that allow for faster information processing. They include mental processes, including availability (recent instances come to mind more easily than distant ones), base-rate judgments (such as assuming a police officer is male because males represent the large majority of all police), and representativeness (such as making a guess based on how typical something is of a larger category). The heuristic aspect of an aha moment is that its suddenness communicates that we can trust it.

Although heuristics can be helpful mental shortcuts, they occasionally lead to incorrect conclusions. A police officer could be someone other than a man. Atypical presentations of disease are not highly representative of that disease category. And—germane to our discussion here—aha moments can be wrong. This realization, that those flashes of insight might not actually be correct, was a major wake-up call for me as a coach.

Kathryn Schulz is a Pulitzer Prize–winning journalist who wrote the intriguing book *Being Wrong*.[9] Among the pithy lessons contained in her book is the provocative idea that people don't necessarily know they are wrong, and their ideas—even the wrongheaded ones—feel true.

This is corroborated by research on aha moments. The Danek and Wiley research team I mentioned earlier explored true and false aha moments.[10] To do so, they had participants try to figure out a range of magic tricks performed by a professional magician. The participants were able to solve about 37 percent of the tricks. Some of these were carefully and slowly figured out, and other solutions arrived in a flash of insight. Of those flashes of insight, 37 percent were wrong.

In another study, researchers employed three hundred participants to solve anagrams in a laboratory.[11] The researchers included a statement such as "*Ithlium* is the lightest of all metals," and the participants had to unscramble the word to figure it out (lithium, in this example). The anagrams were purposefully made on the easier side so that people would be more likely to solve them not by slowly figuring them out but through sudden aha moments. After solving each anagram, the participants were also asked to use a scale to estimate how true they believed the statement of fact to be (in this example, that lithium is actually the lightest of all metals, which it is). The researchers discovered that people in the study were able to successfully solve anagrams about 60 percent of the time. These solutions came through flashes of insight 40 percent of the time. When such flashes occurred, people reported that the facts felt truer than when they slowly figured out a solution, even when the facts were false.

All this research suggests that aha moments feel true even when they are not. I admit, the flashes of insight our clients have about their jobs, health, or work-life balance are distinct from figuring out magic tricks or solving anagrams. I mention these studies not because they are perfect representations of coaching insights but because they point to the conclusion that we should be rethinking the veracity of insights.

Archimedes wasn't 100 percent spot-on in his theories. It turns out there are exceptions to his principle, including pumice, which does not behave like other stones, and sponges, which do not behave like other fibrous objects. He wasn't dead wrong in his insight about buoyancy and density, but his initial insight needed further refinement.

Eureka Coaching

When we discuss aha moments within the context of coaching, we have to balance their potential with their possible limitations. Clients clearly love to experience these breakthrough moments. My concern is that we see these eureka moments as true—like our clients who experience them—even when they may be partially true or completely wrong. In one study, Tracy Robinson and her colleagues examined the experience of aha moments in coaching and found that they occurred in coaching with far greater frequency than in the months preceding the coaching relationship.[12] However, they also found that flashes of insight were linked to subsequent behavior change in only 56 percent of cases.

For this reason, we cannot stop at client insight as the litmus test for coaching success. We know that clients are going to be susceptible to inflating their ratings of coaching based on these pleasant and seemingly true insights that coaching provides. I would argue that coaches need to follow up—likely in later sessions—to inquire about the veracity and usefulness of these insights. Many coaches already begin each session by checking in on earlier accountability. This is the perfect time to revisit earlier eureka moments and ask how clients view them now, days or weeks later. In all likelihood, clients will still like their insight. If the data are any indication, clients will have actually done something with the insight about only half the time.

In the end, I think this idea provides a clear link from one session to the next. Reflection and inquiry provide a rare and valuable space for clients to arrive at new insights. These put a little spring in clients' steps and provide motivation for them to experiment with behavior change between sessions. In the follow-up, we should address not only the behavior change but also the veracity and usefulness of the insight itself. Once that is complete, we can start the cycle all over again.

We might also explore the insight in greater depth at the moment it occurs. It may be that coaches are inclined to defer to insights because clients are typically enthusiastic about them. Even so, we might do well to stay objective and explore the insight further. Research on insight in coaching by Iain Lightfoot suggests that aha moments typically occur twenty to twenty-five minutes into a session and last for about four minutes.[13] Perhaps this handful of minutes is a critical moment for coaches as well as clients.

REFLECT AND EXPERIMENT

- Track your own flashes of insight. Over the course of a week, do ideas come to you suddenly in the shower? Do you have sparks of inspiration during conversations? What do you notice about these?
- In your sessions, observe your clients right after they have an insight. What changes do you notice?
- To what extent do you follow up on client insights in future sessions? Do you ever ask if the client still feels the insight is as true as when it arrived? What are the potential harms or benefits of such a question?

How Curious
Should We Be?

SURPRISINGLY LITTLE research has been done about the personality traits of coaches. I recognize, of course, that we are a heterogeneous bunch and that there will not—and cannot—be a single "coach personality." Even so, you might expect to find some common trends among the people who self-select into our profession. You might find, for example, a higher-than-normal rate of people who have a strong service mentality. You might find a predisposition toward empathy or a higher-than-average ability in verbal communication. The question of coach personality is important in part because research has linked personality to job performance.[1]

One study—conducted in the United Kingdom by Rebecca Jones and her colleagues—reveals some links between personality and coaching.[2] In particular, clients who were more extroverted tended to see coaching as more effective. This study included a relatively small sample, and I would love to see it replicated. Even so, it points us in the direction of considering how personality might be a factor of note in the coaching relationship.

This brings me to the topic of this provocation: curiosity. As coaches, we are often encouraged to be curious and to use this sense of wonder as an engine to drive our questions. My instinct—and I hope yours—is that this advice is generally good. Throughout the years, though, this encouragement has left me scratching my head, curiously wondering the following:

- Is curiosity related to personality? That is, might some people be just naturally more curious than others? If so, what are the implications for training coaches and encouraging them to be curious?
- Are there types of curiosity, or is it a single entity? Whatever the answer to this question, what are the implications for using it in coaching?
- What about client curiosity? Should we be doing something more strategic with that?

What Is Curiosity?

We've all experienced curiosity—a desire to travel to a foreign land, a burning need to know the name of an actor who was in a certain film, the urge to watch an unusual person walk down the sidewalk, the tit-illating feeling that comes before opening a present. Curiosity creeps up all day every day. The dictionary tells us that curiosity is a strong desire to know or learn about something. This definition is adequate: curiosity is a yearning directed at a particular idea or object. Psychologists often use a similar definition. For example, Todd Kashdan and his colleagues describe it as a "predisposition to recognize and search for new knowledge and experiences."[3] This group of researchers further unpacks the psychological experience of curiosity: they argue that people find something curious in one of two instances.

First, people's curiosity is piqued if the object of curiosity is particularly novel, complicated, or challenging. Because of this, traveling to the Eiffel Tower arouses more interest than shopping for soup in your local grocery store. We can also be more mentally engaged with a challenging project at work than with a task that we can perform almost automatically because we have mastered the skills related to it. In essence, the objects of our curiosity vary in how much curiosity they stoke within us. A blank piece of paper arouses somewhat less curiosity than one of Picasso's paintings.

Another instance is when people sense that acquiring new information about the object of curiosity is manageable. This element is less intuitive. In essence, your ability to handle the new information affects your level of curiosity. Not only does the target of our curiosity determine our feelings of interest, but also something about us influences these feelings. If I tell you, for instance, that a festival takes place during which people drop babies off the roof of a building—there really is—you might have any number of reactions. A reaction of horror indicates that you fundamentally don't get what I am referring to and that the practice is so far outside of your existing web of knowledge that you struggle to make sense of it. By contrast, you might have an attitude of "Really? Tell me more! Where is this, and why do they do it?" You'd be eager to learn the history, rationale, and other aspects of this ritual. Psychologists sometimes call this aspect of curiosity *coping potential* and—as the phrase suggests—it refers to our ability to cope with, comprehend, and find a place for new information.

Over the last decade, the Kashdan research team has conducted dozens of studies on curiosity with thousands of people from all over the world. In 2018, they published an assessment that identified five distinct dimensions of curiosity.[4] In 2020, they revised this assessment, making it shorter and more sensitive.[5] Table 15.1 shows how they parse this topic.

I like this framework because it suggests that curiosity is not a monolithic entity. Instead, curiosity might come in flavors. Some folks are socially curious, others are adventurers, and still others are

TABLE 15.1. Dimensions of curiosity

Dimension of curiosity	Explanation
Joyous exploration	Generally enjoying learning, seeking out new situations, and seeing opportunities for growth in challenge
Deprivation sensitivity	Being nagged by an inability to solve a problem, focusing on it (maybe even being kept awake by it), and working relentlessly to find a solution
Distress tolerance	Having the capacity to handle doubt, stress, and surprise to seek out new knowledge
Thrill seeking	Enjoying risk and adventure, even when it is tinged with fear
Overt social curiosity	Enjoying the process of discovering another person, asking them many questions, and finding out why they do what they do
Covert social curiosity	Being the classic eavesdropper—desiring access to the private lives or thoughts of others and observing their behavior, even if no personal interaction occurs with them

fascinated by just about everything. Breaking curiosity into these component parts can be helpful in understanding what "being a curious coach" might mean specifically for you. It shifts the question from "How curious should I be?" to "How should I be curious?"

Curiosity in Coaching

Thought leaders in coaching have considered curiosity a crucial aspect of what we do from the very beginning. Laura Whitworth and her colleagues from the Co-Active Training Institute (CTI), for example, identify curiosity as the foundation of powerful questions.[6] Their sentiment is echoed time and again by scholars and coach trainers all over the world. Unfortunately, relatively little guidance is available on how exactly we are supposed to activate this crucial resource or use it most effectively.

In recent years, I have found the writings of two scholars particularly useful on this point. The first is Christian van Nieuwerburgh, a colleague I often turn to for guidance because he is thoughtful about coaching and definitely does not agree with me on many issues. He argues that questions should be used not to satisfy the curiosity of the coach but rather in service of the client.[7] A coach who asks, "How much would you get paid if you accepted the promotion?" isn't really helping the client all that much. By contrast, a coach who asks, "How important is the pay raise to your decision?" is using curiosity on behalf of the client. In fact, I love the phrase "using curiosity on behalf of the client" because it suggests that clients sometimes enter sessions worried, angry, or frustrated, and—as an uninvolved party—coaches can more easily access curiosity and gift it to their clients. This distinction between curiosity for the coach and curiosity for the client will, I hope, be useful, especially for less experienced coaches.

More experienced coaches might find the writing of Alison Hardingham, a psychologist and coach at the Henley Business School, as useful as I have. Alison offers a provocation of her own: coaching is one of the most asymmetrical relationships possible.[8] Whereas a friendship involves all sorts of give and take, the coaching relationship focuses almost exclusively on the client. As a result, Alison advocates working hard to understand our clients. We have so much there to explore: understanding their motivations, their personal intuitions about making change, their view of the coaching process, their communication and emotional styles, their strengths and weaknesses, and their current desires and perspectives, just to name a few!

Alison suggests that asking curious questions demonstrates our interest and investment to our clients. This point is crucial for at least two reasons. First, *being* curious is not enough. We must *demonstrate* it to our clients for it to have the ameliorative effect we desire. Second—and this is something I find personally challenging—it might be okay to satisfy the coach's curiosity. By way of example, imagine the following dialogue from a coaching session:

> Client: If I take the new role, I will be transferred from Cleveland to Chicago. That part I actually would like a lot since I grew up in the suburbs there.
>
> Coach: No kidding, which suburb?
>
> Client: Oak Park. It's due west of Chicago.
>
> Coach: Sure, where Hemingway was born.
>
> Client: That's right!

I believe that nine out of ten people assessing this coaching session would view this as a distraction from the work of coaching. Certainly, it violates Christian's advice that curiosity should be used for the client and not the coach. In this instance, the client already knows which suburb they grew up in. The coach, by contrast, is the one who gains new information from the question. In this instance, however, we can also clearly see the benefit in the coach's question. As Alison Hardingham suggests, the coach is offering a demonstration of interest and investment. We can reasonably suppose that the client in this example feels positively toward the coach as a result of this exchange. The coach has bothered to show interest and has found some small point of connection.

This realization made me rethink my position on curiosity in coaching. I still agree with the idea that curiosity should benefit the client, but now I have a broader view of what benefits the client. Here

is my list, in order of importance, of the three main benefits of curious questions for the client:

1. The potential for new insight
2. The opportunity to articulate thoughts
3. The demonstration of interest and investment

With regard to the third benefit, I believe that these types of
questions should be used sparingly. Less experienced coaches especially may be vulnerable to asking questions of idle curiosity more
than is beneficial. What's more, these types of questions might be
most useful primarily at the beginning of the coaching relationship.
In recently published research, Erik de Haan and his colleagues find
less evidence than you would guess that the coach-client relationship (the "working alliance") is of critical importance to coaching
effectiveness.[9] Specifically, the de Haan research team find that the
working alliance is especially important in the first and second sessions—according to both clients and coaches—but its importance
diminishes in later sessions.

In the end, coaches might want to veer from the black-and-white
idea that we ought to be curious. Instead, consider when to be curious, how to be curious, and how we demonstrate curiosity.

REFLECT AND EXPERIMENT

- Try asking a question of idle curiosity in a coaching session.
  Observe the effect it has on your client. Is this effect worth
  the question?
- Avoid asking questions that the client might already know
  the answer to or already have a reasonably articulated answer

to. Try to ask questions that are unusual or that the client has not yet considered.

- Reflect on whether you have gone online and looked up more information about baby-dropping festivals. Have you? What does this say about your own curiosity, if anything?

What If We Used Less Empathy?

I SPEND a fair amount of time working with coaches at the beginning or in the early stages of their coaching careers. Some of these people are students who are just beginning their formal training, others are seeking certification, and still others have a couple of years of professional experience under their belts. In observing their coaching, I have arrived at the conclusion that the largest challenge for them is not getting drawn into the client's issue. This tendency is a professional hazard for all of us. We desperately want to serve our clients by facilitating insight, and we can be tempted to want them to solve their problems. Add to that the fact emotions are contagious, and keeping psychological distance and objectivity can be difficult.

To put it another way, our empathy—broadly defined—can act like the powerful gravity of a black hole, pulling us into the client's story, enmeshing us with the client, and making it feel like the client's success or failure is our own. At its most extreme, we can feel tempted to more actively participate in solving the client's problems, such as offering advice. Over time, empathy can also be a predictor of burnout because the coach feels each frustration, disappointment, and irritation of their clients.

Given the fact that, on the one hand, empathy seems to be critical to coaching, and on the other hand, it presents certain risks, what are we to do? Should we advocate for empathy in coaching? Should we suggest using less empathy? The answer depends on what we mean by *empathy*.

Definition of Empathy

I'll admit it: the aspect of psychology I like least is the perennial arguments over defining key terms. If you look at the research literature on well-being, you will find a dozen distinct understandings of the concept, and as many for the concepts of intelligence, optimism, and, yes, empathy. No researcher has the monopoly on the truth, and all the various definitions and assessments combine to create a more robust understanding of the phenomena. I view these varying empirical approaches in the same way that I understand snapshots. Any given photograph of you is not the whole truth. A photo taken at lunch today does not capture your high school graduation, the time you had a fever, or whenever you are in your pajamas and therefore does not offer a complete picture of you. Yet the image of you is real, valid, and a true representation of one side of you. I find it helpful to keep this in mind when I see academics arguing over the nuances of terms such as *well-being* or *empathy*.

With this in mind, I offer a brief overview of empathy informed by a publication I wrote with my colleague Sara Hodges, an empathy researcher at the University of Oregon.[1] I don't claim that this definition is the only way to understand empathy, but I do suggest that this primer is potentially helpful in giving coaches a more nuanced understanding of this topic.

In general, empathy is a psychological process of joining with another person. Empathy includes two distinct elements: an emotional process and a cognitive process. The emotional aspect is what most people think of when they refer to empathy. The common layperson understanding of this side of empathy is feeling what another person feels. By contrast, many scholars divide the emotional part of empathy into two subcategories, referred to as *empathic concern* and *personal distress*:

- *Empathic concern*—This is what many people think of as compassion or sympathy. This category describes feeling *for* another person, such as the experience you have when you find a lost child. You don't spend time trying to figure out the child's experience; you feel concern, and you try to help the child. In coaching, if clients report that they are overwhelmed or experiencing hardship, you are concerned for their well-being.
- *Personal distress*—This is the stereotype many people have of empathy because it means that you are feeling *with* another person. Your own emotional experience mirrors theirs, such as when you curl into a ball while watching a video of someone taking a tumble down some stairs or you tense up when seeing someone jump into a frigid lake. In coaching, if clients report that they are overwhelmed or experiencing hardship, you find yourself feeling the press of overwhelm in your stomach or chest.

The cognitive portion of empathy refers to the mental game of walking a mile in another person's shoes. Also known as *perspective taking*, it is the ability to make a reasonable guess about another person's experience. Perspective taking exists on a continuum that ranges from the straightforward ("the widow is probably thinking about her husband on the anniversary of his death") to the probable ("I think we were invited as a courtesy; the host does not actually want us attending") to the difficult ("What would it be like to live in a refugee camp?"). Research suggests that imagining something from another person's point of view consistently increases empathic concern as well as a sense of overlap between the two people—a sense of *us*.

Taken together, I am partial to this well-developed understanding of empathy. It allows us to elevate our advice from "Use empathy" or "Coaches should be empathic" to something more distinctive. As coaches, we can benefit from employing some perspective taking and empathic concern but not necessarily feeling what our clients feel.

Critiques of Empathy

Empathy holds so much obvious appeal. I don't have to highlight the fact that empathy can lead to cooperation, reduce prejudice, or promote generosity. What I will highlight is the other side of the empathy coin. Empathy also has a number of critiques, and I offer these not to dismiss this attractive concept but to add depth to how we understand, train, and use it within coaching.

The Australian social worker and educator Susan Gair offers a deep reflection on the topic.[2] She asserts that we should be cautious in believing that we can truly understand another person's perspective. She suggests that perspective taking is a combination of how we believe people would generally act combined with a dollop of how we would act in a particular situation. As a result, we can get empathy a bit right but never totally right. At worst, we can get it wrong. It turns out that most people default to imagining how *they* would act in a situation rather than how the other person might. It can lead to more egocentric views. In a study of more than two hundred coaches with an average of thirteen years of experience, researchers found that eleven participants claimed that sharing personal information with their clients was vital.[3] That's eleven too many for me.

I think the distinction between how *we* would act in a situation and how *others* would act in a situation might actually be good news for coaches. It aligns well with our beginner's mind ethos, in which we try not to assume that we know too much about our client. Retaining an attitude of humility where perspective taking is concerned keeps us curious and learning about our clients. I like to think about this as if two-thirds of our perspective taking is silent (access to our own point of view and our understanding of what people in general would experience). The third portion is what our client is actually describing to us, which we then try to learn more about. I'm not suggesting, however, that the first two-thirds are unimportant. I believe that these sources of information are vital for several reasons:

- They can be used as a contrast with the client's experience in instances where they do not match the client's experience.
- They can be used to fast-forward the coaching in instances in which the client's experience dovetails with general experience.
- They can be used by the coach to ask better questions in instances in which the coach has some insight into the experience.

Another criticism of empathy is offered by Robert Elliott and his colleagues.[4] In essence, they argue that—at times—people want emotional distance. Imagine a client who feels a little embarrassed about a recent performance review. They mention it in passing but make an attempt to steer the conversation away. The coach then says, "I see you avoiding the review. It was embarrassing to you, and it is understandable that you might want to shift directions." Nominally, this response is empathic because it accurately identifies the client's internal experience. In many ways, though, it is inappropriate because it seeks to reassure the client (who, in this example, did not ask to be reassured) and it can feel intrusive to the client (who did not want any empathy).

Unwanted empathy is a particularly sticky challenge for coaches. In modern coaching practice, coaches commonly intervene in a variety of ways—to challenge client thinking (as in the case of so-called self-limiting beliefs), offer empathy, and make observations about client processes or behavior. We engage in these practices because they often work well, and we can see tangible client benefits. They might not work all the time, however, but—I have not found any research investigating this. Anecdotally, I have heard coaches describe their clients as "resistant" or "not ready for coaching" because, in the coach's opinion, the clients did not want to face a challenge or truth about themselves. I am not convinced. My instinct is that clients should have the right to open up at a pace that suits them and that coaches—myself included—would do well to remember that our keen observations can hit too close to the bone. Over the last few years, I have made this change in my own practice: I have emphasized promoting more psychological safety for my clients so that when I offer the occasional laser-like observation, they feel less vulnerable and exposed.

A final critique can be found in the many ways that coaches occasionally take credit for client success. Admittedly, I have not read research on this, but we have all experienced it at conferences, during presentations, and in one-on-one interactions. I once saw a well-known coach boast of how a company's revenue increased by a jaw-dropping proportion after it engaged the coach to work with its senior leadership. Even if the brag was accurate (I suspect that more factors besides coaching influenced the organization's bottom-line performance), this anecdote offers an example of empathy gone wrong. In this case, the coach was essentially saying *we* instead of *them*. They were overlapping their identity with that of the company—a form of perspective taking—resulting in their taking credit for the client's success. I often see coaches do this when a client experiences a setback or failure, and the coach subsequently feels that they have somehow let the client down. In the end, the trick is to balance the degree of connection and distance with your clients.

REFLECT AND EXPERIMENT

- How good are you at distinguishing between empathic concern and empathic joining? How do you demonstrate your concern to your client without getting wrapped up in their emotions or story?
- How much do you monitor the self-other distinction in perspective taking? How much do you think "What would a person generally experience in such a situation?" versus "What would I be like in such a situation?" versus "What is my client telling me about their experience of a situation?" We all know that we are *supposed* to do the last of these three, but occasionally slipping into the others is natural.
- It can be beneficial for your clients to remember that unwanted empathy exists. How do you know the extent to which your empathy is being invited and welcomed by your clients?
- To what extent do you feel the ups and downs of your client's outcomes? How can you gain greater distance from these? What is the optimal amount of distance?

Can Assumptions Be a Coaching Tool?

YOU MIGHT know the old joke about assumptions. When one person makes an incorrect assumption, the other asks, "You know what happens when you assume?" and the answer is "You make an *ass* out of *you* and *me*" (which, when put together, spells the word *assume*). Besides this joke not being particularly funny, it has rarely rung true for me. I feel like I make helpful assumptions all the time:

- I assume the sofa in my living room will still be there in the morning.
- I assume that my clients will show up at the agreed upon time.
- I assume that if I exercise, my health will be better.
- I assume that I will be a better coach in the future than I am now.

Everyone—and I mean everyone—makes assumptions from the time they wake up to the time they go to bed. These rough guesses and predictions are vital to helping us function. I don't have to lie in bed, for example, fretting that my sofa might be gone. Assumptions are often correct and provide a rule of thumb for how the world works. Operating on these forms of mental autopilot frees up brain space for us to think about other stuff.

Yet these assumptions are not perfect theories of the world. They are useful but sometimes wrong:

- Although my sofa has always been there in the morning, my bicycle was once stolen out of my living room while I slept.
- My clients have, on occasion, showed up late or not at all for our coaching sessions.
- Although I exercise, I have also sustained sports-related injuries that have hurt my health.
- I might not be a better coach in the future.

Assumptions have two sides: they are powerful templates that help us navigate the world more efficiently, and they can also be biased and incorrect. As coaches, it might make sense for us to reflect on what assumptions really are, what assumptions we carry into our sessions, and how they might impact our coaching.

First, a Caution

I'm going to be honest and say that I am more nervous writing this provocation than I am for most of the others. Although I don't expect every reader to connect with or believe in the content of each provocation in this book, I *assume* that readers will have a somewhat harder time with this one than many of the others. The reason I have developed this particular guess is that I taught social psychology at Portland State University, and I have seen how people often react to this topic. Social psychology is the study of how other people influence our thinking, feeling, and behavior. It can be upsetting because we would generally prefer to think that we are in the driver's seat—acting rationally and intentionally—when much of our behavior is subtly influenced by external forces. By way of example, I often asked my class of 100 students to raise their hands if they felt like they were directly influenced by advertising. Only a handful of arms went up, and I suspect these students weren't actually paying attention. Next, I asked how many students felt advertising was effective on other people, and nearly every hand shot up. I saw this in the fall term and again in the spring, year after year.

The same holds true about us as coaches. As a group of people who have self-selected into this profession, received specific training, and worked hard to improve, we are pretty good at being mindful and aware. Most of us want to think we are present and intentional. If that's what you think, I agree. My provocation here is that we just are not as present, intentional, or aware as we might believe.

Understanding Schemas

What do we mean when we talk about assumptions? A dictionary definition tells us that assumptions are information that we accept as true. Although they have a bad reputation, assumptions are part of our functional psychological architecture. Assumptions help us by saving us from having to test every guess we might make about the world. If I arrive at immigration at Heathrow Airport, I can assume the officer who takes my passport will speak English because it is the national language of England, and this employee works for the government. The assumption saves me having to ask, "Do you speak English?" In other contexts—such as wanting to place an order in a café in Budapest, I am likely to ask the staff if they speak English to ensure I can place my order in that language. This pair of examples illustrates the fact that assumptions are more than bad guesses, biases, and stereotypes; they are a mental scaffolding that tells us how the world works.

One of the most common approaches to understanding the psychology of assumptions is to think of them in terms of schemas.

Schemas are knowledge structures that people use to organize their experiences and guide their decisions. In essence, schemas are like scripts for how situations will likely play out. You have a wedding-based schema that suggests you should say "Congratulations" to the couple rather than "too bad" and that you should bring a gift rather than take one. You have schemas because they help in situations, especially ambiguous ones, which place a higher load on our mental processes. Schemas serve as shortcuts that make our processing more efficient. The downside to this is that these same shortcuts are generalized guesses and not always true of the situation. A small example of this is when I ask my social psychology class to imagine a police officer (go ahead and do it yourself). The overwhelming majority imagine a man because the rates of men in policing are high even though we all know that people other than men who work as police officers. What's more, a surprising number of people imagine police officers in a classic outfit—trousers, button-up shirt, epaulettes, and a hat—even though many modern police wear tactical vests and gear with no hat.

Where coaching is concerned, we need to understand that schemas are not just about whether the assumptions are accurate or not. Schemas guide what we pay attention to and remember. If you have a schema about the mind-body connection, you might be on the lookout for this as you speak with your clients. You might be more likely than other coaches to ask about physical sensations, note physical shifts, or believe that the state of your client's body affects their mood, thinking, and behavior.

One common example of this among coaches is the assumption that all people have self-limiting beliefs. When coaches hear clients say, "I don't think I can do it" or "I'm not good at that," the schema gets activated—the coach understands these statements through the lens of self-limiting beliefs—and focuses the coaching on addressing these thoughts (either through exploring or challenging them or both). Although this mental process can be helpful, the downside is that, like all schemas, it carries an amount of bias. Sometimes clients truly aren't good at certain tasks, and they are being honest and self-aware. I once told a group of coaches that I don't think I will ever be an MCC-level coach (using the ICF designation for master coach). Everyone in the group rushed to challenge and reassure me. "Never say never, Robert," they told me. They clearly heard my statement through this common coach schema. In reality, I keep a very small client load and do not anticipate that I will accumulate the one thousand additional hours of coaching I would need to qualify for MCC. In fact, I am not even working toward that direction. We might all hold self-limiting beliefs, but this is not one of mine. I hope this illustrates the idea that these mental templates are useful but need to be employed with care and intentionality.

Coaches love to reflect and I argue that the topic of assumptions is a terrific one for consideration. What are your assumptions? Do you have working theories about trauma, leadership, well-being, emotion, language, change, and other topics relevant to coaching? You certainly do. In fact, a relatively new topic of research on people's fundamental beliefs about the world and how it operates has been pioneered by Jer Clifton. These beliefs are called *primals*, and his research team has identified three broad categories of beliefs that exist across cultures.[1] Take a look at the three categories in table 17.1 and consider which beliefs within each category you might harbor.

When I reflect on my own primal world beliefs, I see that these ideas are articles of personal faith rather than proven philosophies. I must admit that for every example of abundance I can produce, I acknowledge that a counterexample of scarcity exists. Even so, I cling to my belief in abundance because it makes the experience of living more positive and enjoyable for me. I also see how these assumptions influence my coaching in three different ways.

TABLE 17.1. Primal world beliefs

The world is generally safe	The world is generally enticing	The world is alive
It is progressing (versus declining).	It is abundant (versus scarce or barren).	It needs me (versus it doesn't need me).
It is harmless (versus threatening).	It is meaningful (versus meaningless).	It is interactive (versus indifferent).
It is cooperative (versus competitive).	It is improvable (versus too hard to improve).	It is intentional—things happen for a reason (versus unintentional or random).
It is stable (versus fragile).		
It is just (versus unjust).		

First, these beliefs operate as my fuel source. A belief in abundance, for instance, gives me a degree of positivity and optimism that can serve my clients. I see them as being resourceful people in an abundant world and know that such a world offers more potential for impact and change.

Second, understanding my primals helps me identify potential blind spots. I have a slight leaning for thinking the world is just, for example. I tend to think that bad behavior is punished more than rewarded and that good behavior is rewarded more than punished. Even as I write this, I am aware that I have a privileged background in many ways and that not everyone's experience of justice will match my own.

Jer Clifton has begun investigating the extent to which our primal world beliefs might be based on our unique life experiences.[2] Certainly, life experiences inform our worldviews, but we must avoid the temptation to assume that a person will hold one or another worldview based on our perceptions of their life experience. For example, women do not see the world as more dangerous than men do, people who grow up in lower income households do not see the world as less abundant, and members of higher income families do not necessarily see the world as more abundant. Even so, the research determining the extent to which our worldviews are retrospective (resulting from experience) versus interpretive (a lens to understand experience) is just beginning.

Third, by having a formal vocabulary by which I can understand and discuss assumptions, I am better able to ask my clients questions about their own worldviews. All coaches believe that the client perspective is an important consideration in coaching, and primal beliefs and other assumptions are a powerful tool for exploring this. You might notice that clients wrestle with instances in which their assumptions are violated, such as when acts seem to be random, meaningless, unjust, or getting worse. You can form your questions to explore these assumptions, such as asking the following:

- What do you believe about the world that is being threatened here?
- How long do you believe this state of affairs will last?
- What do you believe about exceptions to rules?
- What have you done in the past when your worldview has been shaken?

In my coaching, I pay particular attention to my clients' causal assumptions. For example, they might tell a story that they are a particular way because of their early childhood experiences or that they have been promoted at work because of their natural talents. They believe these stories fervently and are guided by them. My job as a coach is not necessarily to disabuse my clients of their foundational assumptions but to explore them to shed light on their effects.

Taken together, primals offer a well-articulated and formal vocabulary for understanding the assumptive worldviews that guide our attention and thinking. They are worth considering and using as a lens to better understand ourselves and our clients.

REFLECT AND EXPERIMENT

- Consider your own assumptions. It might even be helpful to write them out as one-sentence thesis statements. What specifically do you believe about change, potential, coaching, emotions, beliefs, embodiment, and other topics relevant to coaching?
- Think about specific coaching interactions you have had. See if you can locate these within the primal world belief framework. Where do you notice a particular client-focused worldview? Where do you see your own creeping into your coaching decisions? What will you do with any insights that arise from these reflections?
- Before your next session, spend a few minutes articulating your basic assumptions and beliefs about the ways that coaching works. Note any limitations or potential benefits that might arise from these assumptions. Use any insights to experiment with your presence and questions and see how this process affects your coaching.

Why Do We Dislike Self-Disclosure?

I HAVE trained coaches for over a decade at Positive Acorn and through other training institutions, and I love observing novices' intuitions about how to coach and the coaching relationship. One common intuition relates to coaches' strategic use of self-disclosure. Experienced coaches will agree that coach self-disclosure is not a large part of coaching. In fact, self-disclosure is generally proscribed. Coach training programs—including my own—recommend against it. In my experience as a trainer, this recommendation fundamentally challenges many people learning how to coach. They strongly desire to disclose personal information just as they feel a strong temptation to give occasional advice.

I see many potential problems with coach self-disclosure. In fact, I once discontinued working with a coach who, during each session, would chime in with a little personal anecdote. I listened patiently, but the whole time I was hungry to get back to talking about my own goals and challenges. I have also seen time and again how novice coaches attempt to use self-disclosure as a way to sneak in their advice. By offering a quick personal anecdote or insight, they subtly suggest a possible course of action to the client.

This push for self-disclosure happens frequently enough that I became curious about it. Why do so many beginners have an intuition that coach self-disclosure is potentially beneficial when so many experienced coaches think the practice is largely unnecessary? To answer this question, I turned to the dozens of coaching books lining the shelves of my office: classics, such as *Co-Active Coaching* and *Coaching for Performance*; foundational books, such as *An Introduction to Coaching Skills*; and highly thoughtful books, such as *Narrative Coaching* and *Coach the Person, Not the Problem*. I was surprised to see that none of them include a reference to self-disclosure in their indices. Not one. Next, I turned to the International Coaching Federation's markers for assessing coach competence. Once again, I didn't see anything specifically prohibiting or dissuading coach self-disclosure.

I found this surprising and wondered if I was alone in thinking that coach self-disclosure was something to generally avoid. I could think of a few instances of colleagues whom I respect admitting to occasionally disclosing something, but those examples seemed to be the exceptions rather than the rule. I found myself scratching my head about this phenomenon so much that I wanted to go back to the drawing board. In an effort to determine why coaches turn up our noses at the idea of self-disclosure, I decided to try to understand it better.

The Social Goals of Self-Disclosure

Social scientists have been studying self-disclosure for ages. They have investigated sexual self-disclosure, self-disclosure on social media, self-disclosure when interacting with artificial intelligence, and self-disclosure in psychotherapy, among many other related topics. Much of this body of research has focused on self-disclosure as a process: why do people do it, and what happens when they do? The answers to these questions most often concern feeling connected to one another or creating a certain type of impression about one's self. Many theories have been proposed to explain why self-disclosure is part of the human communication repertoire:

- *Social exchange*—If we view relationships in economic terms, conversations are exchanges. Disclosing can signal to your conversational partner that you trust or like them and so are willing to divulge personal information.
- *Uncertainty reduction*—When we meet people, we do not know much about them and have to figure them out. We make many judgments about their similarity, warmth, trustworthiness, and likability. The process of disclosing personal information can reduce the uncertainty and fast-forward the bonding process.
- *Information processing*—People want to sort and manage information. We determine what the most important information about other people might be, and we act as gatekeepers for our own information, which is why we don't just self-disclose without a strategy. If you meet someone for the first time, for instance, you might choose to lead with neutral facts ("I work at Intel"), positive facts ("I've been married for twenty-five years"), or targeted negative facts ("I really messed up in my previous relationship, but I learned so much in the process").[1]

These theories provide handy explanations for why self-disclosure is so important to our interactions. In many ways, they set the pace and tone for intimacy between two people. That said, these broad theories concern everyday social exchanges. Professional interactions, by contrast, operate with their own norms and objectives. What works in conversation at a wedding reception is somewhat different than what works in the boardroom.

The closest profession to coaching, in my opinion, is psychotherapy. Fortunately, lots of research literature on therapist self-disclosure is available that might offer insights into our own interactions. Two University of Memphis psychologists reviewed this body of literature and articulated several points:

- Nine out of ten therapists report using personal self-disclosure, and highly experienced therapists do so significantly more than novice therapists.
- Clients do not see self-disclosing therapists as being more trustworthy or empathic than those who do not use self-disclosure. They do, however, see such therapists as being warmer.
- Therapist self-disclosure is linked to more positive client self-disclosures.

Unsurprisingly then, some therapists think that strategic self-disclosure can have potential benefit on the therapeutic process.[2] If, indeed, self-disclosure can be helpful, then it makes sense to consider categories of self-disclosure. Researchers have created a list that I believe is worthy of consideration.[3] It includes the following:

- Biographical information, such as marital status or having children
- The current feelings a person is having in reaction to what is being discussed
- Past experiences a person has had and the lessons learned from them
- Personal approval or legitimization of the other person's experience
- Personal perspectives that serve to challenge the other person to see things in a new way
- Immediate thoughts about how the current interaction is going

When we look at this nuanced list, we can see that perhaps certain types of self-disclosure are common in coaching. For example, a coach might say, "Wow! I am really in awe of the hard work you have put into this." This coach is sharing a personal internal experience, but their goal is to recognize, support, and celebrate the client's efforts. One of the most common critiques I receive when people watch me coach is that I have a tendency to do minor self-disclosures in this vein. I sometimes say, "Oh, I think that's cool!" or even the occasional "I really like that." My critics worry that by making these statements I (1) unnecessarily insert myself, (2) risk making the client dependent on my approval, and (3) risk the possibility that the client will feel judged by me. All these criticisms are fair, and I believe that to address them we have to look at the reasons coaches self-disclose.

Why Coaches Might Self-Disclose

After consideration, I have identified four primary reasons that coaches might engage in self-disclosure with their clients. These observations are my own, and I readily acknowledge that this list might not be complete.

To Be Liked

All people want to be seen in a favorable light and be accepted by others. You see this penchant in coaches in a variety of contexts: coaching websites often have an "About Me" story that showcases the coach as resilient, expert, or empathic. In interactions with other coaches, I notice a leaning toward positive self-presentation. I rarely hear coaches say, "I blew it!" or "I thought I was really paying attention, but it turns out I missed critical information." Finally, in coaching sessions, coaches occasionally mention personal details that are intended to promote likability. For instance, they might say, "Wow, I cannot even imagine what that must have been like for you," which is both an attempt to validate the client's experience but also a signal that the coach is humble and respectful. My attitude is that this rationale for self-disclosure in coaching is not strong enough to justify doing it.

To Bond or Connect

My instinct is that this form of coach self-disclosure is most common. I see coaches reveal personal details in an effort to connect with their clients: they disclose similar experiences to signal to clients that they understand the client ("I get you, I also lived in London for a while"), and they disclose personal emotions to signal to the client that they are impacted by the client ("I find myself smiling just hearing you say that").

My attitude here is that this form of self-disclosure can occasionally be helpful in coaching. I don't think that sharing a personal experience in the session is particularly beneficial, although I see the initial session as a possible exception to this. By contrast, I do see the benefits of sharing personal emotions and reactions. These types of self-disclosures communicate to the client that you are present and invested. In the absence of coach emotion, powerful questions become interrogations. In fact, my feelings about this are so strong that I believe that sharing momentary emotions is a more powerful form of active listening than giving summaries, which coaches so frequently do with their clients.

To Help the Client

This form of self-disclosure is perhaps the second most common one. I know that novice coaches often self-disclose to help their clients, and I am curious how often more seasoned professionals do it as well. In this category, coaches disclose personal experiences that contain lessons or advice for the client. I once heard a coach say to their client, "I also used to be a micromanager. Then, I just experimented for a week to see what it would be like if I didn't give any input. I was surprised by what a relief it was and how well everyone else performed in my absence." Although this personal anecdote was certainly well-intentioned, it steered the conversation in the coach's preferred direction, robbed the client of the opportunity to arrive at their own insights, and promoted one solution—the coach's—over others.

I generally believe that this type of coach self-disclosure is most harmful and, interestingly, is one of two main types that clients invite (the other being bonding or connecting disclosures). In my experience both as a coach and coach trainer, clients ask for direct suggestions surprisingly often. Sometimes, these requests are framed as "What should I do?" but just as often, they come in the form of "What would you do?" We can feel tempted to answer, and sidestepping such requests with grace can be challenging. Even so, a coach demonstrates a lack of faith in the client when they provide an answer without the client having a go first. I say *first* because I am open to the possibility that experienced coaches with a great coach-client relationship might occasionally offer advice to good effect. Even so, I believe that this advice—if it ever is offered at all—is best positioned as a consideration rather than as a personal anecdote

Coaches have access to an alternative to self-disclosure besides the disguised-advice version described above. They can instead offer their own personal perspective on an issue, such as saying, "I think that honesty is always the best policy." At first glance, it might appear that this is also disguised advice. It may be, but it is very mild self-disclosure in that it doesn't reveal too much about the coach. It can be easily revised as a thesis to which a client can respond. Imagine, for instance, that the coach said, "If someone said to you, 'Honesty is the best policy,' how would you react?" Here, the coach is stopping short of a personal endorsement and offering the observation for client consideration. This example suggests the broader point that even minor self-disclosures can be reconstituted as useful interventions when we extract the self-disclosure portion.

To Provide Feedback

Coaches are part of the coaching system and can use themselves as a mechanism for offering client feedback. With the client's permission, a coach might reveal their perspective on the client. "You sound defensive when you say that" is the same as saying, "I think you sound defensive when you say that." Coaches do this all the time: we tell our clients what we are observing, what patterns we notice, and how the client is making us feel. This method is the *softest* form of self-disclosure because coaches are not sharing biographical information but instead their current experience.

In the end, self-disclosure has been one of the most troublesome and challenging aspects of coaching for me. In reading the research and pushing myself to look at coach self-disclosure in a nuanced way, I have come to believe that it can be helpful but often is not. When I think about this topic, I am guided by the questions "What counts as self-disclosure?" "What is my goal in self-disclosure?" and "How might this self-disclosure help or hinder this client?"

REFLECT AND EXPERIMENT

- Consider a client with whom you are currently working. List all the things they know about you. This might include biographical information, aspects of your character, your thoughts and opinions, or other information. How do they know all this about you? Some of it you have overtly offered, and some they have picked up by observing you. Could there be a continuum of self-disclosure? What would the points along it be?
- Think about the six types of self-disclosure. Which of these do you do in your own coaching? Which do you think are helpful (and why)? What are the risks of the others?
- Try experimenting with a strategic and small self-disclosure. Make certain that it has potential to help or support the client or move the session forward. Observe how it feels doing it and how your client reacts.

PART FOUR
Coaching Interventions

SOME coaches do not like to refer to what we call *interventions*. I understand where they're coming from. To them, *intervention* sounds too clinical, such as something a doctor or psychotherapist uses to remedy a problem. Other skeptics buck against the word because it emphasizes coaching tools rather than the relationship or process of coaching itself. Despite these reservations, coaches tend to love tools. They want to learn techniques for dealing with specific problems and get certified in assessments that might open the door to new coaching conversations. If the number of blog posts and questions at conferences is any indication, coaches are hungry for formulas, tips, tricks, and hacks to employ in their coaching.

With this in mind, I created a series of provocations to serve as an invitation to reflect on our attitudes toward tools and how we might use them. Some of the provocations in this part are more general, dealing with all possible interventions rather than a specific tool. You can think of these general approaches as my encouragement for you to create a philosophy of intervention. By contrast, some of the provocations are more targeted to specific tools that coaches commonly use.

This part begins in a general way with the idea of *metainterventions*. These are interventions, such as creating norms within the coaching relationship, that make all subsequent interventions more effective. The next four provocations focus more narrowly on specific coaching approaches: first, we reflect on if and how we might intervene in client emotions. Next, we rethink the common practice of assigning homework to clients at the end of a session. After that, we discuss the extraordinarily common practice of combating or reframing a client's negative thinking. I'll be honest in admitting that I don't know if I *ever* engage in this practice, and my provocation reflects this leaning. Next up is a topic that many coaches have an intuitive sense of but is rarely spoken about explicitly: attentional interventions—which are coaching conversations that are unique opportunities to redirect client attention. The part concludes by expanding to a more generalized approach to intervention: I use high-performing rock climbers as a metaphor for clarifying how we might make our coaching more effective.

What Are Metainterventions?

WHEN I applied to graduate school in psychology, the woman interviewing me asked, "What is psychotherapy?" I tend not to like these types of questions because they are so open to interpretation. It is not lost on me that coaches ask these exact types of questions. In the interview, I replied something along the lines of "It is anything that helps a person successfully navigate psychological hardship." I was proud of myself for all of two seconds, until my interviewer countered, "What you are describing is anything therapeutic. Eating soup or playing basketball could be therapeutic, but they are not psychotherapy." The answer she was looking for, it turns out, was "Psychotherapy is a relationship." I would argue that the answer could just as easily be "Psychotherapy is an intervention."

Simply put, interventions are actions undertaken to improve a situation. Imposing government sanctions, joining twelve-step meetings, hiring a tutor, conducting performance reviews, and taking medication are all examples of interventions. In coaching, many of the specific skills we employ are considered interventions: summarizing, sharing metaphors, asking questions, designing plans, using accountability, and so forth. Each of these has a specific ameliorative goal in mind: to provoke insight, build resilience, or increase motivation. In the coaching profession, we spend a fair amount of time reading books and attending trainings to be able to intervene more effectively with our clients.

When I train coaches, I notice that they are interested in more than simply *how* to intervene. They are also curious about *when* to intervene. When I teach the topic of engaging a client on the topic of their strengths, for instance, people often ask, "When should I do this?" The *when* question is an important consideration that suggests coaching interventions have more to them than the interventions themselves. I see this suggested yet again when I interact with coaches who love their particular interventions. One coach might be a fan of mindfulness and then doubles down on introducing mindfulness to all their clients. Another coach might be attracted to the mind-body connection and uses it heavily in their sessions. These techniques can be powerful but they can also be a case of a coach who has a hammer and then looks at everything as if it were a nail.

As coaches, we can focus more on the context that surrounds the specific intervention. In addition to asking, "What should I do (as a coach)?" we can also ask, "With which clients should I do it?" and "When does it make the most sense to do it?" My provocation here is that we spend too little time considering the metainterventions: the contextual factors that influence the efficacy of our coaching interventions.

Positive Psychology Interventions Research

To better understand interventions, I'd like to take a detour into the world of positive psychology. When I am not working as a coach or writer, I am a positive psychology researcher who focuses especially on investigating well-being across cultures. Positive psychology is an applied science, which means that we are invested not only in understanding what goes right with human psychology—such as times when people are generous or humble—but also in improving people's well-being, generosity, or humility. To this end, researchers in my field have tested many so-called positive interventions. These behaviors are typically small—such as journaling about things for which you are grateful, meditating, or spending money on other people—and reliably boost happiness. I'd like to tell you how these came about and how they evolved over time by giving some themes to use when we reflect on coaching interventions.

Positive interventions started more or less in the 1970s. An early happiness researcher named Michael Fordyce wondered if people could learn to be happier. To investigate this, he created a program of activities—fourteen "fundamentals of happiness"—that people could engage in to boost their spirits.[1] His suggestions included "Keep busy," "Don't worry," "Focus on today," and "Lower your expectations." Across more than half a dozen studies, Michael found that trying these activities did indeed boost happiness, especially relative to a control group. More importantly, he discovered that participants in one condition showed the greatest gains: those who came up with their own list of enjoyable activities. You can teach someone happiness skills, or you can have someone come up with their own happiness program. Both strategies are effective, but the personal control and relevance of the latter approach seem to be marginally better.

This idea—that contextual factors matter—was the seed of a number of studies conducted by my friend Sonja Lyubomirsky and her colleague Kristin Layous.[2] They investigated the existing positive psychology interventions by asking not "Do they work?" but "When do they work?" and "For whom do they work?" They found, for instance, that people generally gain more happiness when they can choose from among positive interventions rather than having them assigned. They also found that people derived more benefit from these activities when they were supported by friends and family members. The results of these studies dovetail with many others that suggest contextual factors, such as religion and culture, act as metainterventions that can affect the potency of interventions.[3]

Where coaching is concerned, we know what works reasonably well—so well, I fear, that we too seldomly go back to the drawing board and challenge our basic assumptions. Although this example might sound extreme, I could imagine coaching someone from an Inuit culture, which does not prioritize asking questions but instead emphasizes sitting together in silence, or working with someone typical of a collectivist culture that focuses on doing one's duty rather than doing what one wants. Instead of asking, "How do you feel about this?"—a question that shows a preference to the subjective experience—I might ask, "What is the correct thing to do in such circumstances?"—a question that prioritizes cultural norms. We are just beginning to understand these contextual factors and how they work, and it is one of the most exciting directions for the future of coaching.

What This Has to Do with Coaching

I began writing about metainterventions over a decade ago.[4] It stemmed from my work in positive psychology generally but my attention to working with strengths in particular. An emerging body of research suggests that identifying and using strengths is beneficial. That said, I was also bumping up against cultural impasses. Some people I worked with in England, Denmark, Japan, and Australia were struggling to take ownership of their strengths. They worried that it would come off as arrogant and perhaps too American. I realized that strengths interventions might still work in coaching, but some groundwork might need to be laid to support this. Over the years, I experimented with many metainterventions, intervening with an eye on making another intervention (strengths, in this case) more effective for the client. Here are some examples:

- In my intake session, I would sometimes mention strengths. I would suggest that in the private confines of the coaching session, speaking openly about strengths would not be considered bragging.
- When discussing strengths with clients, I would sometimes say, "I am curious what you think about this statement: strengths are an opportunity to contribute, not to shine."
- Although it is a little gimmicky, I once placed caution tape over a client's door and said, "Your culture is out there, on the other side of the door. That is where it is important to be humble. In here, we have a different culture. In here, it is important to be honest."
- Occasionally, I have worked with clients to create a "strengths genogram"—a family tree of strengths. By identifying their parents' or siblings' strengths, clients often come to feel less self-conscious about their own. They begin to see strengths as something that everyone has, and they see patterns of family strengths.

In each case, I noticed that clients seemed to relax around the concept of discussing or using their strengths. I also noticed that in each case, my metainterventions were about creating cultural norms within the coaching relationship that supported strengths discussions. I began to see my initial session with clients as a particularly valuable time to establish certain types of cultural norms for the coaching relationship. Over time, I identified various design elements for these temporary cultures.

Rituals and Traditions

Rituals and traditions are important in every culture ranging from that of the Olympic Games to C-suite meetings. In coaching, we might ask, "Does the session begin or end with a predictable action or ritual? What if the client putting away their phone was the signal that the session could start?" I believe coaches have intuitions about rituals and traditions but that often they are not made explicit. As I have become more experienced, I find that I am asking my new clients questions such as "Would you prefer to sit, stand, or walk while we coach?" and "Should we break out a whiteboard for our session today?"

Role Induction

Cultures work well when everyone understands their particular role within them. Being explicit about the role of both the coach and client will be familiar to coaches. Even so, many coaches confine this discussion to explaining the boundaries of coaching to their clients. As I develop as a coach, I pay more attention to roles. Who is in charge of learning capture and note-taking, for instance? I have one creative client who loves to generate ideas, and we have agreed that I will take notes of these while he thinks out loud. In most other cases, my client takes responsibility for recording any important insights by taking their own notes throughout the session.

Contrasting

The idea of contrasting highlights the uniqueness of the coaching space. To some extent the coaching session exists outside space, time, and culture. The client is set apart from the daily pressures of work, the conversational norms of society, and the fast pace of life. Occasionally, being explicit about these contrasts can help settle clients into an open, reflective, and honest state of mind.

Shared Experience

The culture of a coaching relationship emerges automatically through interaction. I've noticed that inside jokes, shared vocabulary, and points of agreement can set the stage for a sense of collective culture. The shared experience of the coaching relationship can pave the way for more effective coaching interventions. For instance, I once had a virtual session during which my camera broke. My client—not wanting to be on screen when I was not—joked about punishing me by turning off her camera. This moment became a go-to for us, and we referenced it as "cameras off," which was shorthand for wanting an equal relationship even if you have to fight to get it.

REFLECT AND EXPERIMENT

- Consider making a list of the cultural norms of your coaching sessions. What are the assumptions you and your clients make about your respective roles, the process, the learning, and so forth?
- Reflect on your initial session. What attention do you give to roles, rituals, or cultural norms? If you were to add greater attention to these areas, what might you add?
- How do you pave the way for coaching interventions to land well with your clients? What specifically do you do?

Should Coaches
Address Emotions?

IN MY experience, coaches rarely mentioned emotion between 2000 and around 2010. That decade was closer, I think, to Coaching 1.0, in which people placed an emphasis on goals, values, and motivation. If emotions emerged in sessions, they were addressed largely in the context of motivation. Since that time, however, I have seen greater attention paid to emotions. The number of publications on the topic in the professional literature has increased, and emotions are a theme commonly addressed in training programs and discussed between coaches.

Elaine Cox, a director at Oxford Brookes University, is a thoughtful scholar of emotions in coaching. I especially like that she says emotions are evident in coaching.[1] She does not try to avoid the topic in coaching and suggests that it naturally emerges in sessions. Perhaps the most obvious examples of this are when coaches acknowledge a client's emotional state or when a coach invites exploration of those emotions. This occurrence is common enough that emotions are now part of the markers that the International Coaching Federation have laid out as evidence of the core competency "listens actively."

Despite the prevalence and potential usefulness of emotions in coaching, I have noticed several biases against emotion both when

I discuss the topic with my colleagues and when I observe sessions. The first is the idea that clients must be in a good mood for coaching to work effectively. Although many coaches don't come right out and say this, their behavior in their sessions says otherwise: any time a coach tries to put a positive spin on a challenging experience (also known as *reframing*), reassure a client, or challenge a negative feeling, they are suggesting that positive emotions are better for coaching than negative ones. The second bias I see is a shying away from wanting to discuss emotion at all, which I frequently see among less experienced coaches. Some coaches may view emotions either as clinical phenomena or aspects of human psychology that are problematic. My provocation here is the idea that emotions are a gold mine of information and are appropriate to coaching.

Basic Psychology of Emotions

Let me start by saying that in my opinion the major distinction between coaching and psychotherapy is that psychotherapists deal primarily with clinical distress, such as marital problems, depression, bipolar illness, and trauma. Emotions, however, are not clinical. They are everyday parts of life, and feeling a bout of sadness or a momentary pang of guilt is not a clinical disorder. This means that emotions are fair game for coaching conversations. As such, understanding a few basic ideas about emotions that have emerged from research can be helpful to coaches.

Mood Is Information

People harbor all sorts of attitudes about feelings. For example, they believe that moods can overwhelm a person, people can get stuck in an emotional state, and feelings undermine logic. Regardless of whether those beliefs are true, social scientists agree that mood is information.

Emotions are signals that tell you about your daily experience.[2] Disappointment is a signal that things are not working out as you hoped. Guilt is a signal that you have violated your own sense of right and wrong. Fear lets you know that a threat is nearby. Surprise is an indication that whatever is happening is a violation of your expectations. Mostly, our emotion system works pretty well. This means that where coaching is concerned, we can simply ask about our clients' feelings:

- What is this emotion telling you?
- What is your relationship with this emotion?
- If this emotion had an agenda, what might it be encouraging you to do?

Emotions Are Useful

Emotions have earned something of a bad reputation. Many people believe that feelings cause them to act irresponsibly or interfere with their logical self. By contrast emotion scholars point to consistent benefits of emotions:

- Emotions prepare us for our behaviors.
- They motivate future behavior.
- They signal our experience to others around us.
- They influence other people.[3]

Simply put, emotions are a resource and should be considered as such. Coaches can discuss them in the same way we discuss skills, values, strengths, and relationships as resources.

Emotions Are Socially Constructed

In psychology, we have recently started to see that emotions are socially constructed. Emotions are not necessarily just individual reactions to life but are created and emerge through various social factors, such as your cultural background and the presence of other people.[4] This explains in part why there isn't just some basic emotion called *anger* that is felt the same by everyone and leads directly to predictable behaviors. Instead, anger leads people to do nothing, lash out verbally, leave and sulk, or throw an object, and the list goes on. What determines each of these behavioral reactions to anger is how people make sense of it in each given situation. People access cultural norms that tell them about what is and is not an appropriate expression of anger, they consider how their behavior will influence other people, and they can contract emotions from others. Coaches can take the conversation on emotion deeper by asking any of the following questions:

- What would be (culturally) appropriate to feel in this situation?
- Who else shares this feeling?
- How does this feeling influence the people around you?

I will conclude this section with a simple note on the terms *positive* and *negative* emotions. When social science researchers use these labels, we are not suggesting that emotions are either good or bad. We use these terms to denote two distinct directions, much in the same way that a battery has positive and negative ends.

Emotions in Coaching

Coaches generally enjoy reflection and self-insight. It makes sense then to understand our own attitudes and biases about emotion. Fortunately, Tatiana Bachkirova and Elaine Cox have surveyed coaches to learn more about this topic as it relates to the coaching process.[5] They discovered distinct categories of attitudes about emotion, which influence how coaches perceive their roles, shown in table 20.1.

In this research, as is also evident in coaching sessions, people often assume that emotions are negative. Participants in this study probably didn't think that love, enthusiasm, and being at peace are problematic. In fact, coaches—especially those who view negative emotions as bad—have strong intuitions that coaching works well when clients are in a good mood. This notion is supported by research from the broaden-and-build theory, in which researchers find that positive emotions tend to broaden a person's resources, such as influencing them to be more social or creative.[6] This belief is also supported in the context of coaching by research conducted by Anthony Grant and Sean O'Connor.[7] In one study, they found that inducing a positive mood or combining a positive mood with a solutions-focused approach to coaching outperformed asking about problems. Specifically, the more upbeat coaching approaches predicted higher self-efficacy, more ideas for action steps, and a higher belief that a solution was near.

In this provocation's concluding "Reflect and Experiment" section I have provided specific prompts about positive and negative emotions for your consideration.

TABLE 20.1. How attitudes about emotions guide coaching

Attitude about emotion	Emotions are problems.	Emotions are inevitable and normal.	Emotions represent forward momentum in coaching.
The perceived role of the coach concerning emotion	The coach helps intervene, shape, manage, normalize, or resolve the emotion.	The coach explores the cause and experience of the emotion.	The coach focuses on the energy and motivation associated with the emotion.

REFLECT AND EXPERIMENT

Negative Emotions

- How comfortable are you with experiencing and withstanding your own negative emotions? How about experiencing and withstanding other people's expressions of negative emotions? How does this relative level of comfort affect your coaching?
- When a client experiences or expresses negative emotions in a session, what do you believe is your primary role as coach? To intervene, to explore, or to harness?
- Choose a single example of a negative emotion, and list the potential problems and benefits associated with this emotion.
- Consider mood as information theory. For each emotion— anger, guilt, jealousy, sadness, and fear—see if you can articulate what the typical message might be.

Positive Emotions

- What do you notice about the sessions you have in which your clients largely experience positive emotions?
- Most coaches want to enter their coaching sessions in a positive emotional state, broadly defined. What do you do to prep yourself emotionally for your sessions? What emotional states are you specifically trying to prepare?
- Imagine you had to compete in a debate in which you argue that positive emotions are more powerful motivators than negative emotions. Do you agree with this thesis? What evidence can you produce to support it? What links can you make between this reflection and your coaching?

Why Shouldn't Clients Have Homework?

LIKE TEACHERS, coaches assign homework. Technically, we do not *assign* these tasks so much as invite clients to create them. I guess you could say that coaches don't assign homework but design it. Most coaching sessions wrap up with the client articulating their learning from the session and then partnering with the coach to design activities that attempt to apply that learning. These out-of-session to-do lists go by many names, but we often refer to them as *homework*. Homework is built into coaching accountability. Questions such as "How will you apply this learning?" "What will you do?" and "When will you do it?" are all crucial features of client growth and learning and are a springboard to coaching accountability.

I have completed my own coaching sessions in exactly this same way and understand the benefit of doing so. The coaching session itself is limited: this conversational technology is good for gaining insights, creating plans, and experiencing support but not much more than that. Coaching sessions are certainly not where the real action happens; it occurs instead in the client's office or other areas of their life. In this way, the coaching session is similar to a pregame pep talk, in which the coach and players come

up with a plan, remember their roles, and pump up their enthusiasm. Then, the players must leave the coach behind, take to the
field, and play the game. This happens between coaching sessions,
where clients do the real work of developing themselves and pursuing their goals.

For as sensible as the homework approach is, I believe it merits
mild reconsideration. My provocation here will be relatively short.
Maybe we should frame the homework carefully, perhaps more carefully than we currently do.

A Look at Homework

Since the word we often use is *homework*, I thought I would begin
by taking a look at real homework in the school setting. I do so in
the hopes that traditional homework might offer some metaphorical
guidance to reflect on the types of homework that occur in coaching.

If you do not have school-aged children, you may not be aware
that a sort of cultural war is brewing over the topic of assigning
children homework.[1] On one hand, homework is associated with
enhanced student learning and achievement. Some types of homework and some amounts of homework are better for some types of
learning in some subjects. Overall, adequate data suggest that homework can enhance learning.[2] On the other side of the debate, skeptics
offer up a variety of critiques:

- Parental involvement is a factor in homework. Families with
  available and supportive parents benefit disproportionately.
- Homework occurs after school hours and often interferes
  with family time, recreation, social development, and other
  important life concerns.
- Homework is sometimes assigned in the wrong amounts:
  instructors don't coordinate, so workloads pile up.

The truth is, people on both sides of the debate have legitimate points, which is why the disagreement endures. For our purposes, it is most useful to consider how the fundamental issues around school-based homework can inform our own reflections of coaching-based homework. Here are some of the major themes:

- *Does the client have social support?*—Oftentimes, homework is designed within the coaching session, where only the coach and client are present. Just because the client is momentarily enthusiastic about the action does not mean that the client's colleagues or family members will be supportive. Good coaches are careful to explore social support with their clients before turning them loose to execute their plan.

- *The client's goal is just one of many*—One potential pitfall of coaching homework is that it can myopically focus on a single client goal, just as school homework is centered around learning and not around fulfilling family obligations or developing skills in recreational pursuits. Good coaches remember to expand and link the goal and homework to the client's wider life vision.

- *Is the homework sized right?*—The excitement of the session agenda can distract from the demands and complexities that wait for the client after the end of the session. Coaches attempt to partner with clients to design realistic homework assignments, but they have no guarantee that they are correctly calibrated.

What's the Alternative?

Nothing I have written up to this point is a strong argument against working with your clients to design between-session actions. Indeed, all I have done is caution that we need to do so carefully. Highly skilled coaches will say, "I do it carefully," and less experienced coaches will say, "Good reminder." I'd like to extend the provocation by telling you that although I spent years working with clients to create homework, I never do that now. In fact, I don't ever use the words *homework, assignment, action,* or *action step* with my clients when discussing what happens after the session is over. Instead, I refer only to *experiments*.

Coaching, in my opinion, is not about clients achieving their goals. That's the client's business. My business is engaging them in a process of self-directed learning. Presumably, they will take these insights and self-knowledge and apply them toward their values, but mostly I am invested in the process of my client's learning. Jonathan Passmore describes homework as well suited to supporting in-session learning by extending opportunities for reflection.[3] For example, he suggests that clients can self-monitor between sessions in an effort to gain self-awareness and practice new skills.

Experiments are procedures used to learn, discover something new, determine which of two things might be better, test a hypothesis, and so on. Framing client postsession action as an experiment highlights the goal of the action: to learn. This purpose is different from what is highlighted in much of coaching homework: to achieve a modicum of success. I might say to a client, "Okay, so you are going to experiment with shorter meetings and see how that affects team energy and performance. Interesting. I am curious to see what you learn from that. If it's appropriate to bring it back into coaching, let me know what insights you gain and what revisions you might have to make." In doing so, I sidestep the implicit notion that the client could succeed or fail at their homework. They only have to learn.

REFLECT AND EXPERIMENT

- How do you refer to the after-session action that often gets designed by the client? How might your language and framing impact your client's view of their objective for this action?
- When you pursue your own goals, do you think of actions in terms of learning, progress, or success? What might be the unique advantages and disadvantages of each of these three frames?
- Try referring to your client's intended actions as an experiment. Emphasize the learning element of this action, and note the client's reaction.

What If You Didn't Send Your Client into Battle?

I RECENTLY asked a number of coaches to describe what they pay attention to and notice in coaching sessions. Sure, we'd all like to say we notice everything, but that is impossible. Coaches have leanings, and attention is a finite resource. As a result, we tend to have patterns in what we notice. One coach might be particularly attuned to language and word choice, another might pay attention to posture and facial expression, and still another might have a knack for noticing what is not being said. One response I see when I observe coaching sessions is the attention coaches give to negative self-talk.

Coaches sometimes call this phenomenon *gremlins*, which describes a wide range of related mental messages that can potentially interfere with motivation and performance. Negative self-talk includes self-statements such as "I can't do it." Coaches also occasionally attend to a related concept: negative self-beliefs, which are the attitudes that act as the foundation for negative self-talk. We also sometimes find ourselves on the prowl for negative self-stories, which are expanded examples of negative self-talk that usually include causal theories and context. Finally, as coaches, we are fairly sensitive to so-called negative emotions that are linked to this type of self-talk: fear, paralysis, apprehension, worry, and guilt.

Taken together, this aspect of coaching is remarkably similar to clinical psychology. Both coaching and psychotherapy can attend to the idea that people have patterns of thinking that not only are distressing but also hold them back from being as successful as they might be otherwise. The supposed solution in the face of these self-critical statements is to challenge, reframe, or otherwise intervene. The idea is that by helping clients shed their limiting beliefs, they will be better positioned to achieve their goals. Although not every coach does this, the practice is common enough.

My provocation here is on the provocative side of provocative: I mostly don't believe that self-limiting beliefs exist. Sure, I accede that in a few instances, people have some pretty dark thoughts along the lines of "I am ugly," "I am unlovable," "I am undeserving," and "I am no good." Mostly, however, I think that most of what we deal with in coaching—I am going to fabricate a statistic of 80 percent—doesn't need to be treated like negative self-talk, even if it sounds like negative self-talk.

Problems with Thinking That Self-Talk Is a Problem

As a coach, client, supervisor, and observer, I have seen countless instances when coaches—including myself—have pounced on negative statements in an effort to change the client's mind: Your client didn't fail; they just learned. They don't have weaknesses; they just have strengths-in-training. They aren't doomed to fail; they should be more optimistic. There are a number of downsides to challenging and reframing these client statements. I will outline four of them here.

Attention to Negative Statements Can Lower the Client's Energy

My colleague Paul Jackson is a noted solutions-focus coach.[1] In some of his trainings, he asks people to share the problems associated with their goals and then discuss the resources and progress associated with their goals. As you might imagine, people feel more enthusiastic, motivated, optimistic, and engaged when talking about what goes right rather than what goes wrong.

Paul's approach is supported by a range of research. One early positive psychology study asked one group of students to track daily hassles and another group to pay attention to daily blessings.[2] The blessings group experienced more life satisfaction, exercised more, were more optimistic, and experienced fewer physical symptoms, such as headaches and sore throats. Similarly, an investigation of teachers who received positive psychology coaching revealed that they enjoyed the confidence, gratitude, and hope associated with a focus on capabilities rather than weaknesses.[3] Although these are just two examples, they offer a sufficient rationale for us to ponder the ratio of attention we give to positive versus negative issues within coaching.

We Sometimes Misinterpret Self-Statements

A number of times as a client, I have made statements that I thought were an accurate reflection of my thinking: "I'm surprised at how easy it was to solve that," "I don't think I'd be very good at that," or "I don't think that would work." In each case, I can remember my coaches wanting to challenge my statement. It felt invalidating to me, and I realized that coaches—myself included—occasionally interpret any negative statement as incorrect or unhelpful.

This reminds me of the professional rock climber Kyra Condie. If you aren't a rock climber, you might not have heard of her. She sports a tattoo on her leg that reads, "You suck. Try harder," and it references herself. I can only imagine many coaches cringing at a client saying, "I suck. I should try harder." Yet Kyra says the tattoo acts as a highly motivating reminder to stay humble and persevere. It seems to work: Kyra competed in the Olympics in climbing.

This viewpoint is in line with research on *defensive pessimists*, people who focus on what can go wrong and plan accordingly. Whereas classic pessimists are paralyzed by their anxiety and underperform, defensive pessimists tend to perform as well as optimists because they harness their anxiety and use it to motivate action. Here's the kicker: if you encourage optimists, they perform better, but if you encourage defensive pessimists, they perform worse because by removing their anxiety, you are removing their motivation.[4] In essence, negative does not always equate to being unhelpful.

Sometimes, These Emotions Are Useful and Should Not Be Changed

I often see coaches attempt to "fix" a negative emotion by reframing or replacing it. Some people assume that others shouldn't feel guilt, boredom, or jealousy. Yet emotions are highly functional.[5] Exploring feelings can be much more powerful and validating than trying to get rid of them.

We Buy into and Reinforce the Idea That the Client Is the Problem

At last, we arrive at the argument that I personally find the most provocative: each time we challenge a client's thinking, beliefs, or statements, we are casting the client as the problem. Something about them, in essence, is broken and needs to be fixed. This sentiment is directly at odds with the pervasive philosophy of coaching that holds that clients are whole and unbroken.

Each time we challenge a client's thought or statement, we essentially tell them that something is off about them. Perhaps without even realizing it, we send them into battle, however, the thing they are trying to defeat is themselves. Any time we are at war with ourselves, we cannot win. I see this in the health aspects of coaching all the time: a client complains that they have a sweet tooth or laments how easily they give into temptation. The coach then partners with them to engineer their life to reduce tempting situations or to bolster and strengthen them in moments of potential weakness. What I seldom see, however, is a coach saying, "You like sweets because they are delicious. You eat them because they are prevalent and socially acceptable. There is absolutely nothing wrong with you." A coach can still work with a client to promote health, of course, but little is to be gained in reinforcing the client's story that their history, personality, or behaviors are broken.

The Alternatives

Instead of sending our clients into battle, trying to overcome weaknesses, fix thoughts, and silence doubt, we can partner with them in ways that are more validating and possibly effective.

Acceptance

Saying that we ought to accept our clients is easy but somewhat harder in practice. Imagine hearing your client say that they are positive their plan will not work out or that they don't feel good at the job for which they routinely receive stellar evaluations. We might be tempted to reassure, challenge, or reframe, all of which convey the message "You are wrong." Alternately, we can simply accept that the client has this perspective and that they have arrived at this conclusion sensibly, even if their statement may not reflect the whole truth.

Exploration

What if, instead of challenging and replacing thoughts, we simply explored them? It can be tempting to conflate exploration and challenge, as in the case of asking, "How did you arrive at this conclusion?" (which might be curiosity but also leaves the door open to the subtle suggestion that the conclusion is incorrect). I mean a true exploration based on the idea that negative self-statements might actually have some value. For instance, imagine the following examples:

- *Statement*—"You just said 'I'll never be more assertive than I am now.' You're a rational, intelligent person. I wonder how that statement is helping you."
- *Feeling*—"You are feeling guilty. Imagine that the guilt was an entity with its own agenda. What do you think the guilt is encouraging you to do?"
- *Behavior*—"You mentioned that you have a tendency to 'beat yourself up.' What is it that being hard on yourself might be trying to accomplish?"

In each of the examples above and in my own experience of coaching, clients typically arrive at productive answers. It turns out that feelings—to the extent that they have an agenda—are encouraging actions that the client values. Many self-defeating statements often protect clients in certain ways.

Partnering

I do not mean the coach partnering with the client but instead the client partnering with themselves. An exploration of thoughts, feelings, and behaviors that assumes benefit instead of brokenness paves the way for clients to accept themselves and quit trying to defeat themselves. I sometimes say to my clients, "What would it be like if you partnered with this [feeling, thought, etc.] instead of working against it? You both seem to want some of the same outcomes. What if you joined forces and worked together?" I find that this approach frees up client energy to focus on their goals rather than making repairs, it engages them with the coaching process because they feel more rather than less resourceful, and they feel more seen and accepted by me.

REFLECT AND EXPERIMENT

- Consider your own view of self-limiting beliefs and negative self-talk. To what extent do you view this as a problem (disordered thinking) versus a technique (self-motivation or protection)?
- To what extent do you believe you can accept negative self-statements in yourself? In your clients? What might help you to accept such talk?
- In your sessions, pay attention to the ratio of time spent discussing resources, values, and goals versus weaknesses, challenges, setbacks, and limiting beliefs. Note how your client reacts to each type of focus.
- Try accepting your client's negative self-talk and exploring how it might be helpful or the purpose it is currently serving. Make certain that you are not challenging it but framing it as acceptable, natural, and useful. See what emerges.

What Are Attentional Interventions?

ATTENTION IS a finite resource, which is why coaches cannot notice everything, although I believe that we are pretty good at noticing details. We have a penchant for noticing physical shifts in our clients as well as language and word choice, and we can pick out themes and values that undergird client statements. Even so, simply too much information is available through too many channels for us to take in and process everything. For instance, we might be oblivious to the discomfort a client from another culture feels in trying to conform to our patterns of communicating.[1] We might not observe what the client is leaving out of a story. We might overlook how we are coming across to the client. The list goes on.

This is true of our clients as well. They notice some things and not others. In fact, having someone else point out what they might be missing is one of the primary benefits of coaching. A large part of coaching is understanding our client's perspective and then directing their attention so that they can gain and benefit from alternative perspectives. When we ask questions, we are fundamentally directing their attention. When a client says, "That's a good question," they are commenting on the fact that they have not recently focused on this particular area of inquiry. In essence, they were not paying attention to it.

My provocation here is that coaching is an attentional intervention. We might even consider it a metaintervention in that clients typically enter a coaching session ready to have their attention redirected. Coaches are directive in that we direct client attention in a variety of ways.

A Little Background on Attention

Before diving into the attentional interventions themselves, let us first linger on the concept of attention itself. Pioneering psychologist William James said that attention was the focusing of consciousness toward one out of many possible objects or trains of thought.[2] James—and the rest of us—purposefully tend to use the word *focus* when discussing attention. Attention works like a spotlight; it can sweep broadly, illuminating the entire landscape, or it can be focused, casting a brighter light in a narrow portion of the landscape.

Although we might consider ourselves as being in conscious control of the spotlight of our attention, most of the attentional processing we do happens below the level of conscious awareness.[3] Every moment of every day we are being bombarded with sensory information. Dogs bark in the distance, planes fly overhead, trees blow in the wind outside our window, empty coasters sit on our desks, we feel the buttons on our computer keyboard and the press of the chair under our legs. We have far more stimulation than we could ever consciously sift through and still have the capacity to get anything done. Therefore, people are built with detectors of sorts that help us sift through information in ways that allow us to ignore it or attend to it, as may be necessary. One example is to be found in the fact that we have neurons specifically for detecting novel sounds and that we have adapted to be able to determine the distance, speed, and direction of moving sounds, all without conscious thought.[4] Non-conscious processing means most of the information that comes at us will not rise to the conscious level of awareness.

In coaching, we attempt to focus the limited resource of our attention on the details that matter: the client's physicality, language choice, emotional expressions, narratives, goals, values, strengths, and others. I believe that coaches are pretty good at focusing on and noticing these dimensions, but we cannot do so all the time. It humbles me to remember that when I am noticing a particular turn of phrase in the moment, I am probably missing a shift in posture or vice versa. Not identifying another detail is not necessarily problematic but just an acknowledgment of our own limited nature. In realizing that we and our clients are typically focusing only on a narrow set of information, we also learn that we can change our attention to shift our perspectives and, ultimately, our understanding.

Attentional Interventions

Perhaps the most common attentional intervention is simply asking a question. Every time we inquire about something, we are redirecting our client's attention to that particular topic. In fact, many coaching interventions are in essence attentional interventions. When you point out a shift in posture to your client or highlight the way they phrased something, you are directing their attention. When you ask what a future self might advise the current client self, you are directing your client's attention from the outside in. Virtually every coaching intervention says, "Hey, look at that!"

It might also be helpful to view attentional interventions—mostly questions—in terms of their expanding and contracting qualities. Expanding attentional interventions tend to be those that look *inside out*—that is, the client is asked about their own internal feelings, thoughts, and perspectives. Good coaches expand out from these psychological states to include physical and somatic states and then to the physical and social environment. By contrast, *outside-in* questions seek to remove clients from their established perspectives and look at themselves from an outside perspective. These so-called *metaviews* can include questions such as "What would your supervisor say if she could hear what you are saying now?" "What would future you advise the current you?" and "If your job could talk, what would it say to you?"

In my experience, outside-in questions tend to stop at the level of the behavioral and cease to contract any further than that. Imagine, however, if you could contract these questions in the same way that you expand the inside-out inquiries from the social to the behavioral and psychological. For example, you could ask the following questions:

- What does your supervisor think of this issue?
- How might your supervisor react if she could hear the way you are discussing this?
- What might your supervisor notice about your language or body as you deal with this issue?
- If your supervisor could affect your inner thoughts and feelings about this issue, what might she want to accomplish? What might be her rationale for that?

Surprise interventions are a distinct and more provocative type of attentional intervention. Surprise is a knowledge emotion that is principally about attention. Surprise occurs when events deviate from your expectations, offering a mental wake-up call that says, "Hey, pay attention here! Something is going on!" Consider the example of driving while on mental autopilot. Perhaps you are on your way to work, dropping children off at after-school lessons, or heading to the gym, and you are zoned out and driving by instinct. Suddenly, a car swerves into your lane and you stomp on the brakes. Your heart races and your adrenaline pumps. Your attention is entirely redirected: you are no longer lost in the reverie of your own thoughts but are focused back on the task of driving.

Coaches can strategically redirect their clients by saying surprising things. These might be puzzling, emotionally powerful, or otherwise veer from the expected script of the coaching session. I have done this many times by saying things like "What about your desk drawer?" or "What about my pocket?" These nonsequiturs seem so out of place that clients come up short. They are puzzled and ask, "Wait. What did you say?" In that moment, they have left behind their emotional overwhelm, pessimism, or whatever it is you are strategically distracting from. I typically follow up by saying, "There is potentially a solution to your problem there" (in your desk drawer or in my pocket). This runs so counter to coaching—the idea that there is a solution hanging out in a physical location or that the coach is about to offer a solution—that clients remain highly engaged. I ask if they are willing to play along and, if granted permission, we pull an object from the desk or an object from my pocket and use it as a metaphor.

It honestly does not matter what the object is. I have used coins, toys, leaves, erasers, sewing kits, reading glasses, keys, acorns, rubber bands, and a wide range of other objects. As long as you and the client have some modicum of ability to work with metaphor, the object doesn't matter. Clients imbue the item with their own significance and I am surprised how often this admittedly hokey technique is a major turning point in the coaching. In my opinion, it isn't because of the metaphor, per se, but because of the emotional distance and refocusing produced by the surprise intervention.

I think we are just beginning to scratch the surface of what surprise can do in a coaching session. A strategic curse word from an otherwise clean-mouthed coach, shifting briefly into a second language, spontaneously turning off video, sending a text message: each of these might rattle a client out of stuck-ness and provide a fruitful change of direction in the session. I have experimented mostly with the one-two punch of "there is a potential solution" and then offering a metaphor. It is exceedingly effective but requires that the surprised client is game to explore an unusual new direction. I have also noticed that some unusual questions can have a similarly surprising effect. I once asked my client, "If your alarm clock could talk, what would it want you to know?" and the quirkiness of the inquiry was engaging to the client. In the end, we know very little about how we might strategically use surprise in our coaching sessions, what the effects might be, and with whom it might work well or be contraindicated. I encourage you to experiment with it. You might be surprised by what you find.

REFLECT AND EXPERIMENT

- Pay attention to surprise in your own life. Are there different types of surprises? How do you typically react to each?
- What does the above reflection suggest to you about how you might apply surprise in your own coaching sessions?
- You likely work with metaphors from time to time. How might you introduce metaphors in new and surprising ways? Try it—take the risk—and see how your clients react. What do you notice?
- What effect does thinking about surprise have on your own engagement with your coaching?

What Is Crux-Focused Coaching?

WHEN I am not engaged in my professional activities, I am a rock climber. Please don't think that this is some chest-thumping brag about my adventurous exploits and feats of derring-do. In fact, I am a mediocre climber, and I confine myself to easier routes. I mention climbing only because it is so relevant to coaching. Climbing is all about self-development, is a highly mental pursuit, requires motivation, and at its core is about overcoming problems. In fact, climbers call routes *problems* because certain sequences of movement, but not others, can unlock them for a successful ascent.

I also think climbing serves as a nice metaphor for coaching. In long routes, two people are involved. The climber is the one who has to do the hard work of scaling the wall and figuring out the route. They must manage their own stress and fear and rely on their own experience, perspective, and strength to make forward progress. The climber is not alone, however. They have a belayer who is on the ground, holding the rope and providing a measure of safety. The belayer has a broader perspective of the whole wall and can, upon request, offer the possibility of insight or shout words of encouragement to the climber. I think this description fits that of a relationship between client and coach.

Given the metaphorical accuracy, I have long been interested in the research literature on climbing and what it might tell us about coaching. Indeed, many studies on climbing focus on the physiological and mental aspects of the sport, as well as on competition, performance, and self-care. This body of research is, in my opinion, an overlooked repository of information that might provide thoughts for consideration for coaches. In this provocation, I suggest that we use select aspects of climbing to inform our coaching.

A Primer on Competition Climbing

To help you better understand the metaphorical significance of climbing, I'd like to quickly bring you up to speed on the nuts and bolts of competition climbing. Like its extreme sport cousins kayaking and mountain biking, competition climbing takes place in an artificial environment. Instead of sending athletes into the forest to look for tall rocks, route setters design indoor climbs using plastic holds on walls of various degrees of overhang.

One discipline within competitive climbing is called *bouldering*. These tricky, powerful routes are designed to mimic boulders you might find outdoors. Because the climbs are relatively short, no ropes are required. If a climber falls, they typically land safely on a mat. The competition begins with a preview period during which the climbers can view the climbs before attempting them. They often use this period to rehearse movement and even discuss various strategies with one another. Then, the climbers attempt the climb one climber at a time, and they get as many attempts as they like within a given time period, such as four minutes. Whichever climber successfully tops the most climbs or achieves the highest point of any climber on the climbs wins.

Elite Performance and Coaching Success

Thanks for bearing with me with all this talk of rock climbing. Even though this sport may not be your cup of tea, I hope you will appreciate what it offers our professional work. I will confine my discussion to two specific instances in which climbing can inform coaching: previewing and a crux focus.

Previewing

As mentioned before, the previewing period of a climbing competition is when the athletes have an opportunity to look at the climbs—or problems—from the ground. Researchers have found that the opportunity to preview is associated with greater success in climbing as well as more efficient movement and process during the climb.[2] When we think about previewing a problem in our own lives, it raises interesting considerations. First, some portion of coaching is about clients previewing their own problems, challenges, or plans. Because coaching often attends to the preferred future, clients have the opportunity to preview their goals and consider the routes to those goals and to do so from the safety of the coaching session—much like a climber getting ready to compete.

Second—and in my opinion, more importantly—a preview session is built right into every coaching session. During the agenda-setting portion, the vast majority of all coaching sessions begin. I am, admittedly, something of an enthusiast of setting agendas. I have seen coaches treat this launching point in surprisingly casual ways, such as asking, "What's coming up for you?" and then just launching into the coaching proper. A look at the International Coaching Federation markers for this competency reveals that coaches can easily do more to set an agenda than determining the topic of conversation.

Good coaches use this early portion of the session to preview—or get the lay of the land—before heading into the main portion of the session. They ask questions such as "In what way is this particular topic important to you?" and "What themes and issues do you anticipate arising as we discuss this topic?" In doing so, they make room for coach and client alike to preview the coaching before it even happens. During this time, the coach gets the backstory, an introduction of key players and themes, and a foreshadowing of the client's language and perspective, all within the opening minutes of the session. Taken together, the answers to these agenda-relevant questions provide the coach a huge amount of useful information so that once they launch into the main part of the coaching, they already have ideas about what to ask, what might arise, and what some of the most fruitful routes for the client might be. When coaches take the time to linger and explore the agenda without rushing to finish it and then starting coaching prematurely, the coaching becomes much more efficient, just like a climber who knows what to expect.

A Crux Focus

Remember, the crux is the hardest part of the climb. Typically, any given climbing route consists of a variety of moves, but one or two might be particularly tricky (do you use your left or right hand next?) or physically demanding. Great climbers don't give equal attention to every single move on a route. They spend disproportionately more time focusing on the crux. One climber put it like this: "I concentrate on the hard parts. The easy places: they take care of themselves."[3]

In much the same way, coaches can fast-forward the action of coaching by focusing especially on crux issues. Time and again in my roles as mentor coach, supervisor, and observer of coaching sessions, I have seen coaches avoid the core issues. Some worry that getting to the important stuff "too soon" will feel intrusive to the client. These coaches feel that they need to warm up and connect, sometimes even for a few sessions, before getting to the crux of the issue! Other coaches simply meander. They are excellent at exploration but seem hell-bent on exploring every related aspect of the agenda without prioritizing the stuff that matters most. I believe that this crux focus is especially important in organizational coaching, in which sessions might be shorter and demand more efficiency.

A specific example of crux-focused coaching is to be found in the first question the coach asks after the agenda is firmly established. For instance, the coach has spent ten minutes setting the agenda. They have asked, "What would you like to be coached on?" "In what ways specifically is this important to you?" "What themes, challenges, or other issues do you anticipate emerging as we coach on this topic?" and "What specifically would you like to have in hand at the conclusion of our session that would be satisfying to you?" Perhaps the client says, "I am wrestling with an out-of-synch team. I just don't know where to start. I cannot tell if the main issue is one somewhat surly team member or if it is getting buy-in from everyone on addressing this problem or if it is just a matter of practicing some better communication. I guess I would like to know how to prioritize these various considerations." Crux-focused coaching looks at that last statement—the thing the client most wants to take away from the session—and places it front and center. In this example, we can already see that the crux of the issue is that the client is uncertain and looking to prioritize by way of reducing uncertainty and presumably increasing their own confidence and motivation. This concern is exactly what the coach ought to start with. Why ask questions such as "What would a good team look like?" when the client has been loud and clear about what they want most? You don't have to worry about those ancillary, exploratory inquiries—as the climber said, "They will take care of themselves." Instead, ask an opening question such as "How would you go about prioritizing them?" or "What would have to happen to bring you greater certainty on this issue?"

Conclusion

You don't have to be a climber or any sort of athlete to be a great coach. Thinking like a climber, however—at least in some instances—might help you to be a great coach. Taking your time to preview the client and their proposed agenda often provides all the information you need and leads to a less reactive coaching session. You might still encounter unexpected twists and turns, but the broad strokes are generally known. You can also do your client the favor of drilling down immediately on only the most crucial matters, trusting your clients to take care of the easier stuff on their own.

REFLECT AND EXPERIMENT

- Consider how you partner to set the session agenda. How long does it take? How many questions do you ask? Perhaps most crucially, how well-informed are you by the time you are done setting the agenda?
- If you considered the agenda-setting portion of your sessions to be preview periods, what changes might you make to how you go about contracting with your clients?
- Reflect on your own attitudes about the critical issues for your clients. To what extent are you comfortable addressing them right away? What are some of the factors that influence your relative level of comfort?

- Experiment with asking about—and to the best of your ability, discerning—the crux issues. What is at the core of your client's coaching agenda? What are the most important themes or issues? Start with those, and see the effect it has on the session and your client.

PART FIVE

In the End

TO round out the number of provocations in this book to twenty-five, I include a bonus reflection asking about the extent to which coaching ought to be informed by science. In my opinion, this idea is the single most provocative one in this book. We live in an age when science is under greater scrutiny and in which more people are skeptical about science than at any time in the last hundred years. Part of this trend is the result of intentional efforts to undermine science. Robert Proctor is a historian at Stanford with expertise in "agnotology"—the cultural production of ignorance. The recent past is full of examples of manipulations of science to cast doubt: Holocaust denialism, skewed uses of data relating to climate change and the health hazards of smoking, and vaccine skepticism are just three examples.

The reputation of science has also taken a hit—at least in my own field of social psychology—as the result of the so-called replication crisis. Many published studies, especially those having to do with priming and other unconscious processes, have not stood up well against the test of time. Modern researchers have been unable to repeat some classic studies with any success. This has led to a number of initiatives to improve the quality of science, but these developments tend to receive less press than the failed replications.

Taken together, these trends mean people have less faith in the scientific method as a way of knowing, which is crucial for coaching because this industry has one foot in science and the other in, well, nonscientific influences. Modern coaching emerged from a variety of personal development disciplines, including encounter groups and techniques from the human potential movement. Although these tools might be effective, they are not scientific (even if they have their roots in science). I'm not disparaging them but simply pointing out that they do not use systematic observation, measurement, and analysis as their primary approach to knowing.

You can see this schism clearly in modern coaching: in the most recent ICF conference I attended, one presenter used representative survey data, and another presenter recommended that the audience listen to verbalizations of monetary amounts as a means of manifesting wealth and success. It's not just the ICF; as a profession, we tend to wrestle with the tension between being inclusive of all ways of knowing and having a preference for scientific scrutiny, between making room for professional intuition and conducting a systematic assessment, and between concepts such as coaching presence and measurable outcomes for a session.

In the end, my provocation is not really a yes or no question but a reflection on the overall role of science as a means to inform coaching and measure its effectiveness.

Should Coaching Be Informed by Science?

BEFORE I was a coach, I was a scientist. I still am. Although I do not hold a full-time university position, I regularly collect data, publish research, act as a peer reviewer, and collaborate with other academics. My research is mostly concentrated on well-being. I have spent time outside the laboratory collecting data from difficult-to-access groups traditionally overlooked by psychologists: Amish farmers, sex workers in Kolkata, Inuit hunters in Greenland, Palestinian peace protesters, tribal people in rural Kenya, people facing houselessness in the United States and Canada, Hispanic college students in California, and the list goes on. I have studied the experience of emotions across cultures, the way that people from various cultures relate to strengths, cultural differences in hospitality, cultural emphases on friendship, generosity across cultures, and many other positive topics. In fact, my insight into the inner workings of when people are at their best—when they are happy, supportive, giving, and empowered—influenced my decision to become a coach.

I did not want to use my expertise to direct people on how to live a more fulfilling life; that would be antithetical to coaching. Rather,

I wanted to do exactly what researchers do: ask great questions that provide an opportunity for illuminating answers. I felt that my knowledge of the inner clockworks of the good life might help me ask more powerful questions. To put it bluntly, my goal as a positive psychology coach is not to make people happier—that should be left to my clients—but to use happiness as a lens for inquiry. In thinking about this subtle but important distinction, I realized that we can gain so much from learning about the ways that coaching and science can interface.

My final provocation in this book is that coaching and science *should* interface. We seem to be going in that direction, but a scientific approach to coaching is in its infancy at best. I want to articulate possibilities for progress on this front.

Ways of Knowing

Lest I come across as a puritan for empiricism, I acknowledge that we have many legitimate ways of knowing besides science. Knowledge can come from faith, common sense, personal experience, received wisdom, or intuition. Each of these sources of knowledge is powerful and valid and can help us make decisions, understand the world, and inform our plans and goals. In addition, each has its own special features and advantages. Faith, for instance, is a uniquely comforting route to understanding the world. Personal experience is highly sensitive to each person's exact circumstances and context. Received wisdom endures because it has proven useful across generations.

Like these, science—as a way of knowing—has a unique set of features and benefits. At its heart, science prizes empirical inquiry, using real-world observation in a systematic way. This means that science contributes to the other ways of knowing:

- *Observability* (and, relatedly, measurability)—This means that opinion, instinct, and other subjective factors have less room to interfere with the process of inquiry.
- *Testability*—Scientists do not just make claims; they make claims based on data. This means that each proposition can be tested, affirmed, revised, or rejected. Thus, science is a dynamic system of knowledge, one that changes as new evidence emerges.
- *Generalizability*—Science deals in broad "truths" and averages. By employing careful and large samples, researchers are able to generalize from a relatively small group of people to the larger population from which they are drawn. Where anecdotal evidence is context-rich and correct in its local accuracy, scientific evidence tells what is mostly true for most people most of the time.
- *Causality*—Amazingly, the scientific method allows us to establish causality. By using experimental and longitudinal designs, we can determine the ways that variables influence one another. This jaw-dropping aspect of science is the reason we can prevent some strokes and heart disease, identify how people die, predict earthquakes, reduce air pollution, and help teams function better.
- *Confidence through replication*—All knowledge feels true to us, but science is unique in establishing confidence by replicating—or repeating—studies to arrive at stronger conclusions. In my own research, for instance, I found that people living in poverty in India had relatively high levels of satisfaction with their social relationships. I repeated this study two years later with a new sample and found the same conclusion.
- *A dynamic system of knowledge*—This is perhaps my favorite aspect of science. Our conclusions change as new and better

evidence emerges. We modify our best understandings or occasionally discard our understandings altogether.

The Current State of Science in Coaching

I applaud the various efforts that leaders in the world of coaching are making toward forging coaching as a scientifically backed profession. The International Coaching Federation, for instance, has a digital research portal where coaches can access relevant research. Many professional coaching organizations host conferences that emphasize science and feature researchers. The British Psychological Society has formed a division for coaching psychology, the first professional organization to formally recognize coaching as a scientifically informed endeavor. Coaching journals publish research and theory on coaching.

Each of these advances is in its early stages, however. Coaching is a young profession, and its research on coaching is only a couple decades old. By contrast, social scientists have been studying happiness in earnest for about fifty years, and we are still scratching the surface. Coaching will benefit from several aspects of scientific research:

- *Greater collaboration between researchers and coaches*— Researchers tend not to need ideas from coaches—they have their own ideas for research questions. But they do need access to coaches and clients who are willing to participate in studies. We would see a dramatic spike in published research if coaches understood how researchers think, if researchers understood how to interface with coaches, and if a formal mechanism for doing so was in place.
- *Grant money for research*—This can come from government, foundations, business, and professional organizations. The

grants need to be large enough to pay for high-quality research.

- *More programs of advanced study in coaching*—A handful of master's degree and doctoral degree programs exist that emphasize researching coaching. This is a terrific start, but it would be nice to see these kinds of programs proliferate to the point that they are standard in top business schools.
- *Scientific-literacy training for coaches*—Many coach training programs do not focus on science. Some that do do so primarily by telling participants about the results of research rather than teaching the fundamentals of science or scientific literacy. This leaves coaches hearing about neuroscience, psychology, organizational scholarship, and other topics but with little ability to distinguish between research designs and the relative merits of each study.

I believe this last point is especially important because coaching is currently also informed by pseudoscience. I have seen people make all sorts of claims about channeling bodily energy, manifesting outcomes with one's intentions, releasing emotional trauma from bodily cells, detecting lies through eye movements, and other topics that are presented as if they are scientific when they are not. Some of these claims are untestable and therefore unscientific, and some have been tested and found to be untrue or ineffectual. In addition to pseudoscience in coaching are approaches I consider "scientific-ish," meaning that they are rooted in legitimate science but are not part of an endeavor to collect top-notch data and publish in top-tier journals. Rather, they tend to cherry-pick findings and synthesize them in ways that seem (and sometimes are) helpful. The main distinctions between these three approaches are listed in table 25.1.

I want to be clear: I recognize that science is not the only way of knowing and that empirically validated approaches to coaching may not be the only effective ones. Even so, I would like to see

TABLE 25.1. A comparison of ways of knowing

	Scientific	Pseudoscientific	Scientific-ish
The role of evidence	People collect as much evidence as possible from diverse samples in a variety of conditions.	People collect evidence that can only be used to support its major claims.	People are interested in creating techniques derived from findings in other areas.
The nature of evidence	Conclusions emerge from evidence, with priority given to the best evidence.	Conclusions are formed and evidence is then gathered to support these conclusions.	Conclusions are based on synthesis of diverse research findings but not necessarily on direct evidence.
Consistency of belief	People are willing to change or modify conclusions as new data emerge.	People are unwilling to change or modify conclusions or theories, and little new data emerge.	People may or may not be willing to revise conclusions.
The role of the community	The scientific community offers ongoing feedback and debate.	The pseudoscience community consists largely of members who believe in the claims and are invested in continuity of belief.	Thought leaders generally consume high-quality research rather than publishing such research in established journals.

fewer concepts positioned under the banner of science when they are either nonscientific, pseudoscientific, or simply a distant nod to science. We cannot trust marketeers to correct this trend, and so it is up to professional organizations and coaches themselves to promote scientific literacy to distinguish scientific approaches from those that masquerade as such.

How Science Can Inform Coaching

I have discussed some general benefits of the scientific approach as a way of knowing. Knowing, however, is only half of the equation. We need to be able to apply science to enhance coaching.[1] I believe we can do so by doing the following:

- *Creating frameworks*—Coaches love frameworks. We tend to be a creative bunch, and virtually all of us have created a two by two chart or a model on the back of a napkin. Scientists do the same thing, but they test the component parts and examine the relation of each piece to the others. In this way, scientific frameworks provide not only a sophisticated vocabulary for describing human phenomena but also a rich understanding of how these phenomena work.
- *Asking better questions*—Researchers and coaches have a love of questions in common. Often, I can rely on my knowledge of research questions to ask my coaching questions. If a client is speaking about motivation, for instance, I can access my scientific frameworks around motivation to ask questions such as "How important is it to you that a task is enjoyable to get it done?" "What is your relationship to deadlines?" and "How important is the judgment of others to your motivation?"
- *Assessing*—I admit, coaches already have a knack for this one. Coaches regularly use a number of assessments—personality, attitude, self-knowledge, and well-being—to inform their

practice. Even so, familiarity with a wider range of assessments might be useful to coaches who want to use before and after measurements or have clients react to survey results.

- *Contrasting*—It can be helpful for the coach to get a sense of the client's unique perspectives and feelings. To understand the relative nature of this uniqueness, however, it is helpful to have a point of comparison. The broad averages that result from research tell us what is *generally* true, but then we adjust from this anchor point to see the extent to which our clients conform to or defy the norm.

- *Studying coaching*—Ultimately, coaches need to study our-selves, not to gather evidence that our personal approach works but to find out what works, for whom, and how.

REFLECT AND EXPERIMENT

- How scientifically literate would you say you are? What is the evidence or rationale for your response? If you were going to improve your scientific literacy, where would you start?
- How do you typically interface with science? Is it through secondary sources, such as popular books, blogs, and TED Talks? Or is it through primary sources, such as published research articles and conference presentations?
- Imagine that you were able to set policy for every coach trainer in the world. How much importance would you place on science within coach training? What specifically might you emphasize?
- In what specific ways does science inform your coaching? Imagine a one to ten scale where one is "Everything is intu-itive" and ten is "I only do things that have been directly tested by researchers." Where are you along this continuum?

Notes

Introduction to the Positive Provocation Framework

1. Jim Gavin, Nicolò Francesco Bernardi, and Elizabeth Thomas, "What Do Coaches Do? A Portrait over Time" (virtual presentation, Converge 21, ICF, October 26–28, 2021).

Provocation 1: Why Is It So Hard to Be a Great Coach?

1. David B. Peterson, "Good to Great Coaching: Accelerating the Journey," in *Advancing Executive Coaching: Setting the Course for Successful Leadership Coaching*, ed. Gina Hernez-Broome and Lisa A. Boyce (Hoboken, NJ: John Wiley & Sons, 2010), 83–102.

2. Carol S. Dweck, *Mindset: The New Psychology of Success* (New York: Random House, 2006).

Provocation 2: Is Coaching Nondirective?

1. Diana W. Stewart, Jeanne M. Gabriele, and Edwin B. Fisher, "Directive Support, Nondirective Support, and Health Behaviors in a Community Sample," *Journal of Behavioral Medicine* 35, no. 5 (2012): 492–499.

2. Michael Bungay Stanier, *The Coaching Habit: Say Less, Ask More & Change the Way You Lead Forever* (Toronto, ON: Box of Crayons Press, 2016).

3. John Whitmore, *Coaching for Performance: Growing Human Potential and Purpose*, 4th ed. (London: Nicholas Brealey, 2009).

4. Christian van Nieuwerburgh, *An Introduction to Coaching Skills: A Practical Guide*, 3rd ed. (London: Sage, 2021).

5. Laura Whitworth, Henry Kinsey-House, and Phil Sandahl, *Co-Active Coaching: New Skills for Coaching People toward Success in Work and Life* (Boston: Davies-Black, 1994).

6. Marcia Reynolds, *Coach the Person, Not the Problem: A Guide to Using Reflective Inquiry* (Oakland: Berrett-Koehler, 2020).

7. Mary Beth O'Neill, *Executive Coaching with Backbone and Heart: A Systems Approach to Engaging Leaders with Their Challenges*, 2nd ed. (San Francisco: Jossey-Bass, 2007).

8. Graham Alexander and Ben Renshaw, *Supercoaching: The Missing Ingredient for High Performance* (New York: Random House Business, 2005).

9. Tina Salter and Judie M. Gannon, "Exploring Shared and Distinctive Aspects of Coaching and Mentoring Approaches through Six Disciplines," *European Journal of Training and Development* 39, no. 5 (2015): 373–392.

10. Anna Dolot, "Non-Directive Communication Techniques in a Coaching Process," *International Journal of Contemporary Management* 17, no. 3 (2018): 77–100.

11. Ian Day, "Balancing Challenge and Support in Coaching," in *The Coaches' Handbook: The Complete Practitioner Guide for Professional Coaches*, ed. Jonathan Passmore (Milton Park, England: Routledge, 2020), 152–164.

12. John Blakey and Ian Day, *Challenging Coaching: Going beyond Traditional Coaching to Face the FACTS* (London: Nicholas Brealey Publishing, 2012).

13. Jeanne Marisa Gabriele et al., "Directive and Nondirective E-coach Support for Weight Loss in Overweight Adults," *Annals of Behavioral Medicine* 41, no. 2 (2011): 252–263.

Provocation 4: Are We Solving Problems or Improving?

1. Marcia Reynolds, *Coach the Person, Not the Problem: A Guide to Using Reflective Inquiry* (Oakland: Berrett-Koehler, 2020).

2. Paul Rozin and Edward B. Royzman, "Negativity Bias, Negativity Dominance, and Contagion," *Personality and Social Psychology Review* 5, no. 4 (2001): 296–320.

3. Daniel Kahneman and Amos Tversky, "Prospect Theory: An Analysis of Decision under Risk," *Econometrica* 47, (1979): 263–291.

4. Tiffany A. Ito and John T. Cacioppo, "The Psychophysiology of Utility Appraisals," in *Well-Being: The Foundations of Hedonic Psychology*, ed. Daniel Kahneman, Ed Diener, and Norbert Schwarz (New York: Russell Sage Foundation, 1999), 470–488.

5. Mary Beth O'Neill, *Executive Coaching with Backbone and Heart: A Systems Approach to Engaging Leaders with Their Challenges*, 2nd ed. (San Francisco: Jossey-Bass, 2007).

6. Anthony M. Grant and Sean O'Connor, "The Differential Effects of Solution-Focused and Problem-Focused Coaching Questions: A Pilot Study

with Implications for Practice," *Industrial and Commercial Training* 42, (2010): 102–111.

7. Anthony M. Grant, "Making Positive Change: A Randomized Study Comparing Solution-Focused vs. Problem-Focused Coaching Questions," *Journal of Systemic Therapies* 31, no. 2 (2012): 21–35.

8. Anthony M. Grant and Sean O'Connor, "Broadening and Building Solution-Focused Coaching: Feeling Good Is Not Enough," *Coaching: An International Journal of Theory, Research and Practice* 11, no. 2 (2018): 165–185.

9. Anthony M. Grant and Benjamin Gerrard, "Comparing Problem-Focused, Solution-Focused and Combined Problem-Focused/Solution-Focused Coaching Approach: Solution-Focused Coaching Questions Mitigate the Negative Impact of Dysfunctional Attitudes," *Coaching: An International Journal of Theory, Research and Practice* 13, no. 1 (2020): 61–77.

Provocation 5: Why Are Ethics So Boring?

1. Aristotle, *Nicomachean Ethics*, trans. W. D. Ross (Chicago: William Benton, 1987).

2. "ICF Code of Ethics," International Coaching Federation, January, 2020, coachingfederation.org/ethics/code-of-ethics.

3. "ICF Code of Ethics."

4. Jonathan Passmore, "Coaching Ethics: Making Ethical Decisions—Novices and Experts," *Coaching Psychologist* 5, no. 1 (2009): 6–10; and Diane Brennan and Leni Wildflower, "Ethics in Coaching," in *The Complete Handbook of Coaching*, 2nd ed., ed. Elaine Cox, Tatiana Bachkirova, and David Clutterbuck (Los Angeles: Sage, 2014), 369–380.

Provocation 6: Should Coaches Study Learning Theory?

1. Elaine Cox, Tatiana Bachkirova, and David Clutterbuck, "Theoretical Traditions and Coaching Genres: Mapping the Territory," *Advances in Developing Human Resources* 16, no. 2 (2014): 139–160.

2. John Whitmore, *Coaching for Performance: Growing Human Potential and Purpose*, 4th ed. (London: Nicholas Brealey, 2009), 10.

Provocation 7: Why Ask Why?

1. Ian Day, "The Urban Myth of the 'Why . . .' Question. Can Coaches Ask 'Why'?" *International Journal of Coaching Psychology* 3, no. 3 (2022): 1–5.

Provocation 8: What's So Great about Interrupting?

1. Emanuel A. Schegloff, "Overlapping Talk and the Organization of Turn-Taking for Conversation," *Language in Society* 29, no. 1 (2000): 1–63.

2. Deborah Tannen, "New York Jewish Conversational Style," *International Journal of the Sociology of Language* 30 (1981): 133–150.

3. Deborah Tannen, *The Argument Culture: Stopping America's War of Words* (New York: Ballantine, 2012).

4. Christian van Nieuwerburgh, *An Introduction to Coaching Skills: A Practical Guide*, 3rd ed. (London: Sage, 2021).

Provocation 9: Whose Language Is It, Anyway?

1. Maya Rossignac-Milon, Federica Pinelli, and E. Tory Higgins, "Shared Reality and Abstraction: The Social Nature of Predictive Models," *Behavioral and Brain Sciences* 43 (2020): 1–30.

Provocation 10: What Are Symmetries in Questioning?

1. Bertram Malle, "Theory of Mind," *Noba Textbook Series: Psychology* (Champaign, IL: DEF Publishers, 2022), noba.to/a8wpytg3.

Provocation 12: What If We Didn't Say Anything at All?

1. Michal Ephratt, "The Functions of Silence," *Journal of Pragmatics* 40, no. 11 (2008): 1909–1938.

2. Vernon Jenson, "Communicative Functions of Silence," *ETCA Review of General Semantics* 30 (1973): 241–257.

3. Annette Fillery-Travis and Elaine Cox, "Researching Coaching," in *The Complete Handbook of Coaching*, 2nd ed., ed. Elaine Cox, Tatiana Bachkirova, and David Clutterbuck (Los Angeles: Sage, 2014), 445–459.

4. Clara E. Hill, Barbara J. Thompson, and Nicholas Ladany, "Therapist Use of Silence in Therapy: A Survey," *Journal of Clinical Psychology* 59, no. 4 (2003): 513–524.

5. David Drake, *Narrative Coaching*, 2nd ed. (Petaluma, CA: CNC Press, 2018).

Provocation 14: Can We Trust Eureka Moments?

1. Anthony M. Grant, "ROI Is a Poor Measure of Coaching Success: Towards a More Holistic Approach Using a Well-Being and Engagement

Framework," *Coaching: An International Journal of Theory, Research and Practice* 5, no. 2 (2012): 74–85.

2. F. K. Tia Moin and C. van Nieuwerburgh, "The Experience of Positive Psychology Coaching following Unconscious Bias Training: An Interpretative Phenomenological Analysis," *International Journal of Evidence Based Coaching and Mentoring* 19, no. 1 (2021): 74–89.

3. Cornelia Lucey and Christian van Nieuwerburgh, "'More Willing to Carry On in the Face of Adversity': How Beginner Teachers Facing Challenging Circumstances Experience Positive Psychology Coaching. An Interpretative Phenomenological Analysis," *Coaching: An International Journal of Theory, Research and Practice* 14, no. 1 (2021): 62–77.

4. Alexandra J. S. Fouracres and Christian van Nieuwerburgh, "The Lived Experience of Self-Identifying Character Strengths through Coaching: An Interpretative Phenomenological Analysis," *International Journal of Evidence Based Coaching and Mentoring* 18, no. 1 (2020): 43–56.

5. Leticia Mosteo, Alexander Chekanov, and Juan Rovira de Osso, "Executive Coaching: An Exploration of the Coachee's Perceived Value," *Leadership & Organization Development Journal* 42, no. 8 (2021): 1241–1253.

6. Amory H. Danek and Jennifer Wiley, "What about False Insights? Deconstructing the Aha! Experience along Its Multiple Dimensions for Correct and Incorrect Solutions Separately," *Frontiers in Psychology* 7 (2017): 2077.

7. Sascha Topolinski and Rolf Reber, "Gaining Insight into the 'Aha' Experience," *Current Directions in Psychological Science* 19, no. 6 (2010): 402–405.

8. Ruben Laukkonen et al., "Eureka Heuristic: How Feelings of Insight Signal the Quality of a New Idea," PsyArXiv (2018).

9. Kathryn Schulz, *Being Wrong: Adventures in the Margin of Error* (London: Granta Books, 2011).

10. Danek and Wiley, "What about False Insights?", 2017.

11. Ruben Laukkonen et al., "The Dark Side of Eureka: Artificially Induced Aha Moments Make Facts Feel True," *Cognition* 196 (2018): 1–6.

12. Tracy Robinson, Don Morrow, and Michael R. Miller, "From Aha to Ta-Dah: Insights during Life Coaching and the Link to Behaviour Change," *Coaching: An International Journal of Theory, Research and Practice* 11, no. 1 (2018): 3–15.

13. Iain Lightfoot, "Insight Events in Coaching Sessions," *International Journal of Evidence Based Coaching and Mentoring* 13 (2019): 94–101.

Provocation 15: How Curious Should We Be?

1. David J. Holman and David J. Hughes, "Transactions between Big-5 Personality Traits and Job Characteristics across 20 Years," *Journal of Occupational and Organizational Psychology* 94, no. 3 (2021): 762–788.

2. Rebecca J. Jones, Stephen A. Woods, and Emily Hutchinson, "The Influence of the Five Factor Model of Personality on the Perceived Effectiveness of Executive Coaching," *International Journal of Evidence Based Coaching and Mentoring* 12, no. 2 (2014): 109–118.

3. Todd B. Kashdan et al., "The Five-Dimensional Curiosity Scale: Capturing the Bandwidth of Curiosity and Identifying Four Unique Subgroups of Curious People," *Journal of Research in Personality* 73 (2018): 130–149.

4. Kashdan et al., "The Five-Dimensional Curiosity Scale."

5. Todd B. Kashdan et al., "The Five-Dimensional Curiosity Scale Revised (5DCR): Briefer Subscales while Separating Overt and Covert Social Curiosity," *Personality and Individual Differences* 157 (2020): 109836.

6. Laura Whitworth, Henry Kinsey-House, and Phil Sandahl, *Co-Active Coaching: New Skills for Coaching People toward Success in Work and Life* (Boston: Davies-Black, 1994).

7. Christian van Nieuwerburgh, *An Introduction to Coaching Skills: A Practical Guide*, 3rd ed. (London: Sage, 2021).

8. Alison Hardingham, "Understanding Your Clients," in *The Coaches' Handbook: The Complete Practitioner Guide for Professional Coaches*, ed. Jonathan Passmore (Milton Park, England: Routledge, 2020), 48–57.

9. Erik de Haan, Joanna Molyn, and Viktor O. Nilsson, "New Findings on the Effectiveness of the Coaching Relationship: Time to Think Differently about Active Ingredients?" *Consulting Psychology Journal: Practice and Research* 72, no. 3 (2020): 155–167.

Provocation 16: What If We Used Less Empathy?

1. Sara D. Hodges and Robert Biswas-Diener, "Balancing the Empathy Expense Account: Strategies for Regulating Empathic Response," in *Empathy in Mental Illness*, ed. Tom F. D. Farrow and Peter W. R. Woodruff (Cambridge: Cambridge University Press, 2007), 389–407.

2. Susan Gair, "Walking a Mile in Another Person's Shoes: Contemplating Limitations and Learning on the Road to Accurate Empathy," *Advances in Social Work and Welfare Education* 10 (2008): 19–29.

3. Sandra J. Diller et al., "How to Show Empathy as a Coach: The Effects of Coaches' Imagine-Self versus Imagine-Other Empathy on the Client's Self-Change and Coaching Outcome," *Current Psychology* (2021): 1–19.

4. Robert Elliott et al., "Empathy," in *Psychotherapy Relationships That Work*, 2nd ed., ed. John C. Norcross (Oxford: Oxford University Press, 2011), 132–152.

Provocation 17: Can Assumptions Be a Coaching Tool?

1. Jeremy D. W. Clifton et al., "Primal World Beliefs," *Psychological Assessment* 31, no. 1 (2019): 82–99.

2. Jeremy D. W. Clifton, "Testing If Primal World Beliefs Reflect Experiences—or at Least Some Experiences Identified Ad Hoc," *Frontiers in Psychology* 11 (2020): 1145.

Provocation 18: Why Do We Dislike Self-Disclosure?

1. Susan Sprecher, Stanislav Treger, and Joshua D. Wondra, "Effects of Self-Disclosure Role on Liking, Closeness, and Other Impressions in Get-Acquainted Interactions," *Journal of Social and Personal Relationships* 30, no. 4 (2013): 497–514.

2. Sharon Ziv-Beiman, "Therapist Self-Disclosure as an Integrative Intervention," *Journal of Psychotherapy Integration* 23, no. 1 (2013): 59–74.

3. Clara E. Hill and Sarah Knox, "Self-Disclosure," in *Psychotherapy Relationships That Work: Therapist Contributions and Responsiveness to Patients*, ed. John C. Norcross (New York: Oxford University Press, 2002), 255–265.

Provocation 19: What Are Metainterventions?

1. Michael W. Fordyce, "Development of a Program to Increase Personal Happiness," *Journal of Counseling Psychology* 24, no. 6 (1977): 511–520.

2. Sonja Lyubomirsky and Kristin Layous, "How Do Simple Positive Activities Increase Well-Being?" *Current Directions in Psychological Science* 22, no. 1 (2013): 57–62.

3. Lilian J. Shin et al., "Good for Self or Good for Others? The Well-Being Benefits of Kindness in Two Cultures Depend on How the Kindness Is Framed," *Journal of Positive Psychology* 15, no. 6 (2020): 795–805; David

H. Rosmarin et al., "Grateful to God or Just Plain Grateful? A Comparison of Religious and General Gratitude," *Journal of Positive Psychology* 6, no. 5 (2011): 389–396.

4. Robert Biswas-Diener and Nadezhda Lyubchik, "Microculture as a Contextual Positive Psychology Intervention," in *Mindfulness, Acceptance, and Positive Psychology: The Seven Pillars of Well-Being,* ed. Todd B. Kashdan and Joseph V. Ciarrochi (Oakland: New Harbinger, 2013), 194–214.

Provocation 20: Should Coaches Address Emotions?

1. Elaine Cox, "Working with Emotions in Coaching," in *The Sage Handbook of Coaching*, ed. Tatiana Bachkirova, Gordon Spence, and David Drake (Los Angeles: Sage, 2017), 272–290.

2. Norbert Schwarz and Gerald L. Clore, "Mood as Information: 20 Years Later," *Psychological Inquiry* 14, no. 3–4 (2003): 296–303.

3. Hyisung Hwang and David Matsumoto, "Functions of Emotions," in *Noba Textbook Series: Psychology,* ed. Robert Biswas-Diener and Ed Diener (Champaign, IL: DEF Publishers, 2022), noba.to/w64szjxu.

4. Lisa Feldman Barrett, *How Emotions Are Made: The Secret Life of the Brain* (Clerkenwell: Pan Macmillan, 2017); and Batja Mesquita, *Between Us: How Cultures Create Emotions* (New York: W. W. Norton, 2022).

5. Tatiana Bachkirova and Elaine Cox, "Coaching with Emotion in Organisations: Investigation of Personal Theories," *Leadership & Organization Development Journal* 28, no. 7 (2007): 600–612.

6. Barbara L. Fredrickson, "The Broaden-and-Build Theory of Positive Emotions," *Philosophical Transactions of the Royal Society of London. Series B: Biological Sciences* 359, no. 1449 (2004): 1367–1377.

7. Anthony M. Grant and Sean A. O'Connor, "Broadening and Building Solution-Focused Coaching: Feeling Good Is Not Enough," *Coaching: An International Journal of Theory, Research and Practice* 11, no. 2 (2018): 165–185.

Provocation 21: Why Shouldn't Clients Have Homework?

1. Alfie Kohn, *The Homework Myth: Why Our Kids Get Too Much of a Bad Thing* (Boston: Da Capo Lifelong Books, 2006).

2. Harris Cooper, "Homework: What the Research Says. Research Brief," National Council of Teachers of Mathematics (2008): 1–3.

3. Jonathan Passmore, "An Integrative Model for Executive Coaching," *Consulting Psychology Journal: Practice and Research* 59, no. 1 (2007): 68–78.

Provocation 22: What If You Didn't Send Your Client into Battle?

1. Paul Z. Jackson and Mark McKergow, *Solutions Focus* (London: Nicholas Brealey, 2007).

2. Robert A. Emmons and Michael E. McCullough, "Counting Blessings versus Burdens: An Experimental Investigation of Gratitude and Subjective Well-Being in Daily Life," *Journal of Personality and Social Psychology* 84, no. 2 (2003): 377–389.

3. Cornelia Lucey and Christian van Nieuwerburgh, "'More Willing to Carry On in the Face of Adversity': How Beginner Teachers Facing Challenging Circumstances Experience Positive Psychology Coaching. An Interpretative Phenomenological Analysis," *Coaching: An International Journal of Theory, Research and Practice* 14, no. 1 (2021): 62–77.

4. Julie K. Norem and Nancy Cantor, "Defensive Pessimism: Harnessing Anxiety as Motivation," *Journal of Personality and Social Psychology* 51, no. 6 (1986): 1208–1217.

5. Robert W. Levenson, "The Intrapersonal Functions of Emotion," *Cognition & Emotion* 13, no. 5 (1999): 481–504; and Roy F. Baumeister et al., "How Emotion Shapes Behavior: Feedback, Anticipation, and Reflection, Rather Than Direct Causation," *Personality and Social Psychology Review* 11, no. 2 (2007): 167–203.

Provocation 23: What Are Attentional Interventions?

1. Y. William, C. van Nieuwerburgh, and M. Barr, "Exploring Western Coaching Experiences of Japanese Coaches: An IPA Study," *International Journal of Evidence Based Coaching and Mentoring* 17, no. 2 (2019): 52–63; and Silvia King and Christian van Nieuwerburgh, "How Emirati Muslims Experience Coaching: An IPA Study," *Middle East Journal of Positive Psychology* 6 (2020): 73–96.

2. William James, *The Principles of Psychology* (Cambridge: Harvard University Press, 1890/1983).

3. Frances Friedrich, "Attention," in *Noba Textbook Series: Psychology*, ed. Robert Biswas-Diener and Ed Diener (Champaign, IL: DEF Publishers, 2022), noba.to/uv9x8df5.

4. David Perez-Gonzales, M. Malmierca, and E. Covey, "Novelty Detector Neurons in the Mammalian Auditory Midbrain," *European Journal of Neuroscience* 22 (2005): 2879–2885.

Provocation 24: What Is Crux-Focused Coaching?

1. Artur Magiera et al., "The Structure of Performance of a Sport Rock Climber," *Journal of Human Kinetics* 36 (2013): 107–117.

2. Jesús Morenas et al., "Influence of On-Sight and Flash Climbing Styles on Advanced Climbers' Route Completion for Bouldering," *International Journal of Environmental Research and Public Health* 18, no. 23 (2021): 12594; and Xavier Sanchez et al., "Efficacy of Pre-ascent Climbing Route Visual Inspection in Indoor Sport Climbing," *Scandinavian Journal of Medicine & Science in Sports* 22, no. 1 (2012): 67–72.

3. Xavier Sanchez et al., "Identification of Parameters That Predict Sport Climbing Performance," *Frontiers in Psychology* 10 (2019): 1294.

Bonus Provocation: Should Coaching Be Informed by Science?

1. Here are a number of reading recommendations for anyone interested in increasing their scientific literacy. All of these are drawn from Noba, an openly licensed resource that you can freely access (as an added bonus, they will not sell your information). Noba is intended to provide expert-authored, easy-to-read information on the science of psychology appropriate for college-level readership.

Beth Chance and Allan Rossman, "Statistical Thinking," in *Noba Textbook Series: Psychology*, ed. Robert Biswas-Diener and Ed Diener (Champaign, IL: DEF Publishers, 2022), noba.to/uv9x8df5.

Ed Diener and Robert Biswas-Diener, "The Replication Crisis in Psychology," in *Noba Textbook Series: Psychology*, ed. Robert Biswas-Diener and Ed Diener (Champaign, IL: DEF Publishers, 2022), noba.to/uv9x8df5.

Rajiv Jhangiani, "Research Methods in Social Psychology," in *Noba Textbook Series: Psychology*, ed. Robert Biswas-Diener and Ed Diener (Champaign, IL: DEF Publishers, 2022), noba.to/uv9x8df5.

Erin I. Smith, "Thinking Like a Psychological Scientist," in *Noba Textbook Series: Psychology*, ed. Robert Biswas-Diener and Ed Diener (Champaign, IL: DEF Publishers, 2022), noba.to/uv9x8df5.

Acknowledgments

ALTHOUGH A single name often appears on the cover of a book, a publication is the product of many people. *Positive Provocation* is no exception. BK Publishers is special: it is more like a family than a corporation, and I was delighted with the personal touch I received from people in leadership, marketing, editorial, and design. I would like to extend special thanks to my editor, Sarah Modlin, who championed this concept and supported me through the entire process. Thanks also to Ashley Ingram, with whom I had fun judging this book by its cover.

Several colleagues were also instrumental in shaping my thinking about *Positive Provocation* and some of them read early drafts of this work and provided invaluable feedback and debate: Christian van Nieuwerburgh, Carol Kauffman, Michael Bungay Stanier, Laura Mantell, Imogen Maresch, Mark Mathia, Andrea Chilcote, Kim Wasson, and Mary Kay Chess. Thanks also to the six cohorts of my Advanced Practice of Positive Psychology Coaching course, with whom I have deepened my understanding of the inner clockworks of coaching.

Thanks to Nadezhda (Nadia) Lyubchik, who organizes my thinking and who has, for years, made me more effective than I would otherwise be.

Last and certainly not least, thanks to my wife, who supported, encouraged, and positively provoked me all along the way.

Index

acceptance, 165–166
agendas, 18–22
agnotology, 181
aha moments. *See* eureka moments
Alexander, Graham, 11
American Alpine Club, 43
analysis, levels of, 57–58
anger, 153
anticipatory set, 49
Aristotle, 37
Association for Coaching, 41
assumptions
   as coaching tool, 124, 126–130
   definition of, 125
   primal world beliefs and, 127–130
   schemas and, 125–127
   usefulness of, 123–124
attention
   conscious awareness and,
      169–170
   definition of, 169
   directing, with questions, 168–
      169, 170–171
   as finite resource, 161, 168, 170
attentional interventions, 142,
   170–173

Bachkirova, Tatiana, 46, 153
behaviorism, 47, 48

beliefs
   primal world, 127–130
   self-limiting, 126–127, 161–167
blank slate theory, 47, 48
boredom, 49
bouldering, 175
British Psychological Society, 186
Buckingham, Marcus, xiii

causality, 185
challenge
   continuum of, x–xi
   and support in coaching, 15
clarification, asking for, 64–65
clients
   accepting, 165–166
   communicating with, 53–54
   goals of, 158, 159
   homework and, 32, 156–159
   observing, 168
   partnering with themselves,
      166–167
   as the problem, 164–165
   resistant, 121
   social support for, 158
   using language of, 68–69, 70
Clifton, Jer, 127
climbing, as metaphor for
   coaching, 174–179

203

About the Author

DR. ROBERT BISWAS-DIENER is a thought leader in coaching. For nearly two decades, he has applied his research expertise in areas such as well-being, culture, and strengths to the coaching endeavor. In doing so, he is widely regarded as one of the pioneers of positive psychology coaching. Robert has also trained professionals in twenty-five nations in sectors as diverse as banking, policing, education, healthcare, and defense. He also trains coaches from around the world at his ICF-accredited school, Positive Acorn. Robert lives in Portland, Oregon, where he enjoys drawing and rock climbing.

Dear reader,

Thank you for picking up this book and welcome to the worldwide BK community! You're joining a special group of people who have come together to create positive change in their lives, organizations, and communities.

What's BK all about?

Our mission is to connect people and ideas to create a world that works for all.

Why? Our communities, organizations, and lives get bogged down by old paradigms of self-interest, exclusion, hierarchy, and privilege. But we believe that can change. That's why we seek the leading experts on these challenges—and share their actionable ideas with you.

A welcome gift

To help you get started, we'd like to offer you a **free copy** of one of our bestselling ebooks:

www.bkconnection.com/welcome

When you claim your **free ebook**, you'll also be subscribed to our blog.

Our freshest insights

Access the best new tools and ideas for leaders at all levels on our blog at ideas.bkconnection.com.

Sincerely,

Your friends at Berrett-Koehler